"At last, a book with fresh reporting and nuanced insight on the LGBT community in Africa. Corey-Boulet launches the reader into the fight for the rights of queer Africans, with thoughtful attention to the global and local dynamics of activism across cultures. Even better, he gives us more stories of ordinary African lives, animating them with context and charm. This is an important book."

Dayo Olopade, author of *The Bright Continent: Breaking Rules and Making Change in Modern Africa*

"In Africa, gay rights—like most other human rights —exist in a tenuous state, merely tolerated in the best of times, violently repressed in the worst. But beneath the surface, gay lives go on, and unique forms of gay culture thrive even in hostile environments, as Robbie Corey-Boulet writes in this vivid and important book. Their voices are heard in *Loves Falls On Us*, loudly and irreverently, revealing surprising truths about Africa —and the people who misjudge it from afar."

Andrew Rice, author of *The Teeth May Smile But the Heart Does Not Forget*

"*Love Falls On Us* offers moving accounts of LGBT Africans' lives and loves, while demystifying the complexity of gender and sexual diversity politics on the continent. This book is a must-read for anyone interested in LGBT rights and activism."

Ashley Currier, author of *Politicizing Sex in Contemporary Africa and Out in Africa*

"This book provides a gripping portrait of queer life in West Africa, and an intimate insight into the resilience, courage and creativity of those who are marginalized, not only by societal norms of gender and sexuality, but also by global narratives of LGBT rights."

Adriaan Van Klinken, Associate Professor of Religion and African Studies, University of Leeds

"Robbie is a meticulous researcher with an unparalleled knowledge of LGBT rights in Africa, a deep connection with local activists, and an understanding of the complex relationship between well-intended outside human rights groups and the local activist community."

Corinne Dufka, Human Rights Watch, Associate Director, West Africa

"Explores with nuance and sophistication the paradoxical effects of transnational LGBT rights activism."

Graeme Reid, LGBT Programme Director, Human Rights Watch

"An immensely readable, complex, and sophisticated work that is at once heart-wrenching and hopeful. Corey-Boulet delivers the eloquence of top-notch reporting paired with the long-term, thoughtful engagement of an ethnographic study."

Matthew Thomann, Assistant Professor, Department of Anthropology

LOVE
FALLS
ON US

About the author

Robbie Corey-Boulet has worked for over a decade as a journalist, primarily in West Africa and Southeast Asia. He reported for several years for the West Africa bureau of the Associated Press, and his writing has been published by outlets including The Atlantic, Guernica, World Policy Journal and The Guardian. He has also worked in Liberia as a media trainer for the NGO Journalists for Human Rights. He is currently the senior editor of World Politics Review and is based in Brooklyn, New York.

LOVE FALLS ON US

A Story of American Ideas and African LGBT Lives

ROBBIE COREY-BOULET

ZED

Love Falls On Us: A Story of American Ideas and African LGBT Lives was first published in 2019 by Zed Books Ltd, The Foundry, 17 Oval Way, London SE11 5RR, UK.

www.zedbooks.net

Typeset in ITC Galliard by seagulls.net
Index by Liz Fawcett
Cover design by Steve Marking
Cover photo © Marcus Rose, Panos Pictures

A catalogue record for this book is available from the British Library

ISBN 978-1-78699-708-1 hb
ISBN 978-1-78699-518-6 pdf
ISBN 978-1-78699-519-3 epub
ISBN 978-1-78699-520-9 mobi

Printed and bound by CPI Group (UK) Ltd, Croydon CR0 4YY

Contents

Part 3: Liberia

Acknowledgments

The original, very hazy idea for this book emerged from conversations with friends in Nairobi in 2011, before I had ever set foot in any of the countries where the book would ultimately be set. A small army of relatives, friends, colleagues and institutions helped guide me from those initial conversations to this final product, and I'll name many of them here.

The nature of this project, however, stipulates that most of the people in Cameroon, Côte d'Ivoire and Liberia who were most helpful can't be named without being put at risk. This book is dedicated to them. I am profoundly grateful for the trust they placed in me, and for the patience and generosity they brought to our discussions.

This book would not exist without the Institute of Current World Affairs, which awarded me a two-year research and writing fellowship in 2014. Nearly ninety years old at the time, the institute had never before funded work on anything related to alternative sexualities, but the support I received was immediate and sustaining. My champions there included Catherine Rielly, Carol Rose, Andrew Rice, Kay Dilday, Ellen Kozak, Leena Khan and Peter Bird Martin. At various stages of the reporting process, I also received financial assistance from the Investigative Fund at the Nation Institute, the International Reporting Project and New America's Global Gender Parity Initiative.

I first traveled to West Africa thanks to Rachel Pulfer, who gave me a job in Liberia with Journalists for Human Rights. In that role, I had the best colleagues I could have hoped for in Stephen Binda, Saye Messah, Bonnie Allen and Taz Ford.

At the Associated Press, Rukmini Callimachi provided encouragement and space to report on LGBT rights in the region even when there were, at least in the eyes of the bosses, more pressing stories to cover. It was a joy to work with her and rest of the AP Dakar family: my dear friend Krista Larson, Maliki Ouedraogo, the late Francis Eddoh, Ndeye Sene, Carley Petesch, Baba Ahmed, Brahima Ouedraogo, Michelle Faul and Jonathan Paye-Layleh. Throughout the region, in Senegal, Liberia, Côte d'Ivoire, Burkina Faso and elsewhere, I had the privilege of working alongside a deep roster of talented journalists, including Anne Look, Aurélie Fontaine, Olivier Monnier, Émilie Régnier, Drew Hinshaw and Laura Burke.

Matthew Thomann provided my first introductions to the *branchés* of Abidjan, kick-starting a reporting journey that would take over my life. I've been lucky enough to count him as a friend and sounding board for the better part of a decade now, and he generously read much of the early manuscript. Ian Corey-Boulet, Clair MacDougall and Andrew Green also gave careful, thoughtful feedback that improved these pages immensely. I have also benefited from the expertise of Basile Ndjio, Vinh-Kim Nguyen, Stephanie Horton, Neela Ghoshal, Graeme Reid, Matt Wells,

Korto Williams and Ashley Currier, among others. It goes without saying—but I'll say anyway—that any remaining problems and errors are mine.

Kim Walker and rest of the team at Zed Books believed in this project from the moment I brought it to them, and seemed to understand instinctively the value in looking beyond headlines and horror stories. Their enthusiasm got me through the writing. I am grateful to Katherine Flynn for her early interest and guidance.

Judah Grunstein, Hampton Stephens and Freddy Deknatel have created an ideal work home at *World Politics Review* for the past two years. Katherine Guerra and Cabrie Kearns, meanwhile, have helped me make a home out of New York, pulling me away from my desk at just the right time more often than they realize.

Lastly, and most importantly, none of my work would be possible without the love and support of my family: Warren, Will, Ian, Makaela, Amy, Dad, Abby, Harper, Graham, GMB, Bill and, above everyone else, my mom, the inimitable Barbara Corey, who deserves all the credit for any good thing I ever do.

* * *

Portions of Chapters 5, 11, 13 and 15 have been published, in different forms, by Al Jazeera America (5); OPENSpace and TheAtlantic.com (11); *World Policy Journal* (13 and 15); and *World Politics Review* (5 and 15).

Introduction

The tickets promised a 9 p.m. start, but as the hour approached midnight guests were still filing into the villa in Abidjan's Deux Plateaux neighborhood. There were boys who'd paired top hats with skinny jeans, or pastel blazers with gold-colored chains. Others had worn women's clothing for the occasion, covering their scalps in bleached-blond wigs and squeezing into dresses that stopped at mid-thigh. In a look that betrayed just how high the fashion stakes seemed to be, one of the shorter boys put every inch of his stubby little legs to work, pulling black leather short shorts over a pair of gauzy tights that ran down to his sneakers.

The fifth annual Miss Woubi beauty pageant, held on a cool Friday night in early October 2014, ultimately drew a far bigger crowd than could be accommodated by the 100 plastic chairs laid out on the villa's lawn. They came in groups of three or four over the course of several hours, triple-kissing in greeting and looking one another up and down before taking their seats. The evening's MC, a skinny gay boy with a flat top, made few apologies for the delay.

Mocking those worried about the time, he urged them to run home to their wives.

"Tonight we'll see the chic, the glamour," he declared, and he would soon be proved right. But first, a quick vocabulary lesson: Non-heterosexual men in Côte d'Ivoire —the West African country of which Abidjan is the largest city, the capital in all but name—use several words to describe themselves. *Branché* is an umbrella term, applying to everyone. Relationships, or couplings of any kind, tend to reflect the heteronormativity that prevails in Ivorian society writ large: *yossis*, meaning men who are "masculine" and "play the role of the man" both in bed and in public, pair off with *woubis*, men who are "feminine" and "play the role of the woman."

Many *woubis*, despite basking in their "femininity," identify as male and present as men in most situations. Yet the Miss Woubi pageant is a special occasion. Once the 2014 event began, fourteen contestants, many of them *woubis* who'd assumed women's names for the evening, paraded down a lumpy red carpet in bathing suits and ball gowns as the sound system blared hits from Nigeria's Wizboy and Congo's Fally Ipupa. In a scene charged with youth and sex and beauty, some maintained their brisk strides as they walked down and back, while others lingered at the runway's end, looking each member of the six-judge panel square in the eyes.

Miss Woubi is the brainchild of David,[1] a portly clothing designer with a raspy voice who proudly identifies as a *woubi* himself. He organized the first pageant in 2009, relying largely on donations from friends to rent out the Cercle du Rail, a now-defunct events hall in central Abidjan. "I knew that if I won or even if I didn't, it would raise my spirits," one participant from that year recalls. "What I loved most of all was seeing my friends to my right and my left."

Word of the pageant spread, and it soon came to occupy a hallowed position in the social calendar of Ivorian sexual minorities. The official motto, according to David, is: "We transform ourselves to realize our dreams." He is proud that the pageant exposes *branchés* to aspects of queer culture they've never encountered. "There are *branchés* who have never seen that who come to see it," he says. "It's an evening where many things can happen: meetings, exchanges, the sharing of information. These elements ensure that Miss Woubi stands out from other parties."

For several years, the pageant took place without incident. In 2011, when the city was still reeling from a months-long post-election conflict that ended with the incumbent president's ouster and arrest, police supervised the event to make sure everyone would be safe. In 2012, however, Miss Woubi's charmed existence came to an end. That year, despite a strict prohibition on all forms of photography, the weekly tabloid *Allo Police* got its hands on pictures of David and some of the contestants. It published these with a story that carried the front-page headline: "The *pédés* of Abidjan have elected their Miss" (*pédé* is a pejorative French slang word that refers to a homosexual man, deriving from pederast or pedophile). *L'Arc-en-Ciel*, another paper, ran a front-page headline that read, "Miss *Pédé* election launched in Abidjan."

"That panicked the *branchés* a little," David said, describing the fallout. He canceled the event in 2013 so the buzz would die down, making the 2014 edition of Miss Woubi the first since the unwanted press coverage. The risk of exposure had hung heavy over discussions of the pageant in the days leading up to it. Yet those in attendance had concluded that the security risks were worth taking, and that they wouldn't be intimidated into staying home.

Once everyone had finally taken their seats, the evening began with a song. Julie, who placed third in Miss Woubi 2012, took the microphone and stood before the crowd, her hair pulled back in a loose bun, her sleeved, floral dress evocative of springtime. Backed by a piano recording, she put her right hand to her chest and launched into "*Hymne à l'amour*," the song Edith Piaf co-wrote for her lover, the boxing champion Marcel Cerdan, and first performed just weeks before he died in a plane crash on his way to see her in New York. Julie sang with range and precision, slowly drawing out her airy French Rs. The crowd responded with approving roars. "*Tu es belle!*" a heavyset *woubi* sitting in the fourth row shouted, over and over. "*Voilà*," the MC said when Julie finished. "That's the strength of *branchés*."

* * *

A few months earlier, an American man in his thirties named Neal Gottlieb, the founder of an organic ice cream company based in Petaluma, California, traveled more than 9,000 miles to Uganda, on the other side of the continent. This was before Gottlieb would become well-known to American television viewers as a cast member of "Survivor," yet he already possessed the self-involvement and flair for self-promotion typical of reality stars.

His mission in Uganda was to climb to the country's highest point, Mount Stanley's Margherita Peak, a feat that took him six days. At the top, he planted a rainbow gay pride flag, an act that, in a Facebook post dated April 23, he said was done "in protest of Uganda's recent criminalization of homosexuality."

In the same Facebook post, Gottlieb included the text of an open letter to President Yoweri Museveni:

> Your country's highest point is no longer its soil, its snow or a summit marker, but rather a gay pride flag waving brilliantly, shining down from above as a sign of protest and hope on behalf of the many thousands of Ugandans that you seek to repress and the many more that understand the hideous nature of your repressive legislation.

He went on to taunt Museveni, who was sixty-nine years old at the time: "If you don't like said flag on your highest peak, I urge you to climb up and take it down. However, you are an old man and surely the six-day climb through the steep muddy bogs and up the mountain's glaciers is well beyond your physical ability."

Gottlieb's trip was apparently inspired by the Anti-Homosexuality Act, which Museveni had signed into law in February 2014. Same-sex sexual acts have long been criminalized in Uganda under colonial-era laws prohibiting "unnatural offenses" and "indecent practices." But the Anti-Homosexuality Act had raised the possibility that penalties even more extreme than jail would soon be meted out. In its original form, it had called for the death penalty for "aggravated homosexuality," a term referring to things like engaging in same-sex sexual acts while HIV-positive or being "a serial offender." By 2014, that provision had been modified to call for life imprisonment, but the law's passage nevertheless sparked an intense global outcry.

A few weeks after Gottlieb returned from Uganda, the Associated Press reported that a court in Kampala, the capital, had opened hearings in the case of the first two men to be tried for homosexuality since the law came into effect. The couple had been arrested "as they fled an angry mob." The following week, Human Rights Watch and Amnesty International released a report documenting a host of abuses committed against Ugandan sexual minorities in the previous few months, including arbitrary arrests and police violence. Researchers had interviewed ten people who were evicted by their landlords, including one lesbian who received the following note from hers: "You have been nice to me and paying very well. But due to the existing situation in the country plus your behavior with your friends, forgive me to suspect you of being indecent, I cannot allow you to rent my house, I cannot fight the government." According to the report, "the most evident impact" of the law had been the "significant uprooting of LGBTI [lesbian, gay, bisexual, transgender and intersex] people," many of whom had fallen into homelessness, gone into hiding within Uganda or fled the country altogether (Human Rights Watch and Amnesty International 2014).

Meanwhile, back in California, Gottlieb was being hailed as a conquering hero (some sample comments on his Facebook post: "Amazing!," "Amazing!!!," "Amazing!!!!!!!," "This is the best thing that has ever happened"). His victory lap involved a round of media interviews. "I could think of no better way to really stand up and make the issue known," he told the northern California radio station KQED.

Yet the coverage also made clear that Gottlieb had conceived of and executed his Uganda adventure without any input from the people he was purportedly trying to help. Some journalists were sympathetic to this approach. KQED wrote that he told no one of his plans "because he feared the ramifications, both for himself and the LGBT community in Uganda" (Jonassen 2014). Never mind that he may well have succeeded in hardening the perception among many Ugandans that people like Gottlieb—meaning white Westerners—are the very ones forcing the "importation" of alternative sexualities into their country. And never mind that, in claiming Ugandan sexual minorities' fight as his own, Gottlieb inevitably brought more attention to them, potentially depriving even the most discreet among them of their ability to maintain a low profile.

KQED acknowledged that, as more people learned what Gottlieb had done, he had come in for some "unexpected criticism." But Gottlieb seemed unruffled by it. He took this criticism merely as evidence that people had strong feelings about LGBT rights issues, while contending that his tactics were as valid as anyone else's. "A number of people have said that this doesn't fit within the guidelines. And as an inexperienced activist, I wasn't necessarily aware that there was a set of guidelines," Gottlieb said. "But as I am learning more and more about the activism surrounding this issue, it's very much a divided group of passionate, caring people that want to see this go away but see different ways to make this go away."

* * *

I began working in sub-Saharan Africa in 2011, moving first to Nairobi on a grant that supported my reporting on transitional justice initiatives stemming from Kenya's 2007–08 post-election violence. I had never freelanced before, and in the months and years that followed I paid close attention to which stories were of interest to international publications—the ones I wanted to write for—and which were not.

By the time I heard about Neal Gottlieb's trip to Uganda, I was not surprised to learn that it had already been covered by places like Buzzfeed and the *Huffington Post*. It seemed to check all the customary boxes for a particular kind of story about Africa, in which a foreigner arrives with half-formed ideas about helping people who are pitied but never consulted, invoked but never heard from. The intentions of the foreigners in these stories are generally assumed to be good, or at least good enough to compensate for any flaws in their plans.

Even before Gottlieb inserted himself into the story, Uganda's Anti-Homosexuality Act had received an extraordinary amount of global attention. The role of American evangelicals, including the notorious hatemonger Scott Lively, in shaping the legislation had further increased American interest in the plight of sexual minorities there. Moreover, Museveni had signed the legislation the day after the conclusion of the Winter Olympics in Sochi, Russia, which had provided an opportunity for international LGBT rights activists, outraged by a Russian law against gay "propaganda," to stoke public concern about the conditions facing sexual minorities the world over.

As a result, the news out of Uganda has played a central role in shaping global perceptions of how sexual minorities are treated across the African continent. But as often happens when an extreme case becomes a stand-in for a much wider experience, this has, at best, done little to enhance outsiders' understanding of the position of sexual minorities in African societies. At worst, the focus on Uganda has placed that understanding out of reach.

Around the time Gottlieb went public with his open letter, I embarked on a two-year fellowship, funded by the Institute of Current World Affairs, to report on LGBT issues in West and Central Africa, parts of the continent where they were receiving relatively scant attention. Almost from the beginning, I saw how the type of coverage generated by a stunt like Gottlieb's clashed with the facts on the ground.

In city after city, country after country, the people I interviewed, be they open or not, activists or not, described complex experiences falling at various points on a continuum between rejection and affirmation. Those who were committed to promoting the rights of sexual minorities went about this work in a variety of ways—some of them visible, many of them discreet. While some took it upon themselves to directly confront the political and religious leaders who threatened their freedom and safety, others devoted their time and energy to activities like the Miss Woubi pageant that offered a chance for people to explore and celebrate their identities. In all cases, it was clear they were not waiting for people they'd never heard of to come in and do the work for them.

This is not to say, however, that foreigners should be written out of the broader story of sexual minority activist movements in sub-Saharan Africa, or that their interventions have always been unwelcome. To the contrary, these movements have been influenced in innumerable ways by foreign money, language and strategies, and any account of their evolution should grapple with that influence. This is especially true in light of the prominent role LGBT issues have assumed in the foreign policies of Western democracies, a development underscored by then-Secretary of State Hillary Clinton's declaration, in a 2011 speech at the Human Rights Council in Geneva, that "gay rights are human rights and human rights are gay rights."

The reporting in this book—from Cameroon, Côte d'Ivoire and Liberia—represents an attempt to tell a version of this story. It is by no means a complete or comprehensive version; in dealing with something as layered as sexuality, comprehensiveness is a fantasy. The point, rather, is to shed light on aspects of the story that should get more attention than they do, as they have more and better lessons to offer than what does get covered.

The first section begins by chronicling how sexual minorities in Cameroon responded to an unexpected upswell of homophobia in 2005 that manifested in raids and, in the case of eleven men in Yaoundé, the capital, incarceration and prosecution. But the story does not end there. Instead, it describes how one of the eleven, Lambert, rebuilt his life once he was released, eschewing opportunities to seek asylum abroad and devoting himself to improving conditions for sexual minorities in his home country.

The second section concerns an Ivorian man named Brahima, who has slept with men for much of his life but has never identified as gay or bisexual, and who has steered clear of activist movements and organizations that increasingly require members to assume such identities. Men like Brahima, who marry women, have children and are often described as living "double lives," endure many of the hardships associated with homophobia in their home countries while remaining on the margins of activist movements that have failed, by and large, to engage them.

The third section describes how gay and bisexual men; lesbians and bisexual women; and transgender women in Liberia, historically the closest US ally in West Africa, have been affected by shifting positions on LGBT rights under the Obama and Trump administrations. It shows how they were caught off-guard, and in some cases endangered, by the Obama administration's decision to openly champion the rights of sexual minorities abroad in 2011. And it shows how they recovered from the backlash, learning over time how to make savvy use of the resources provided by outsiders to navigate spikes in political homophobia, including during Liberia's 2017 presidential campaign.

Finally, it shows how Liberian sexual minorities have been helped and harmed by their relationships with foreign governments and NGOs, and why they have ultimately concluded that they need, one day, to stand fully on their own.

PART 1
CAMEROON

1

Indomitable
lions

On the third Sunday in May 2005, in the early evening, Stéphane hurried his boyfriend out the door so they would arrive before the tables filled up at Victoire Bar, a roadside dive in the Essos neighborhood of Yaoundé, the capital of Cameroon.

Sunday nights at the Victoire offered one of the few regular meeting points for the city's secretive but closely knit community of men who identified as gay or bisexual—or who, regardless of how they identified, had sex with other men. Stéphane, a twenty-two-year-old waiter, had been a fixture of that community for several years, and he tried not to miss a Sunday at the Victoire if he could help it. "It became like a custom," he says. "If you weren't there on a Sunday night, it meant you were sick."

The crowd this particular evening, as was typical, cut across age and class lines. There were college students and fashion designers; boys in their teens and men in their fifties; Yaoundé natives and out-of-towners who'd driven from hundreds of miles away. "There were always new people you'd never seen," Stéphane says.

Those who arrived early enough, Stéphane among them, claimed space on benches and chairs positioned around tables just outside the front door. The rest of the crowd, which numbered in the dozens, stood around the tables or inside, passing around cigarettes and dancing to the French and American pop songs that came through the bar's weak speakers.

When the first police truck pulled up, many of the men assumed it was an ordinary raid, the kind they had witnessed countless times. The officers would enter, demand to speak to the owner, inspect the bar's permits and, after identifying some kind of problem, some minor violation of some little-known rule, demand a bribe before leaving. "They do it a lot in this country," says Didier, a graduate student who'd arrived with a friend about an hour after sundown.

But this time, instead of asking patrons to leave, as would normally happen, the police locked the men inside and began interrogating them, forcing many to lie on the bar's dirt floor. In the confusion, Didier thought for a moment that the officers were going to rob everyone at gunpoint. Instead, they started going from person to person, checking IDs.

Two police vans appeared outside. Lambert, a thirty-year-old IT technician who had been calmly sipping his second beer of the evening when the raid began, asked one of the officers what was happening. The officer said they were looking for someone, without specifying who or why. Then, without explanation, the officers instructed everyone who hadn't managed to flee—about thirty men in total—to board the vans. Only when the men arrived at a nearby police station were they told they were being arrested on suspicion of committing "homosexual acts."

Stéphane, Didier, Lambert and the others could have been excused for their surprise. Cameroon's penal code has criminalized same-sex sexual acts since 1972; Article 347 bis stipulates that such acts are punishable with fines of between 20,000 and 200,000 CFA francs (between roughly $40 and $400), and prison terms of between six months and five years. Yet until 2005, the law was hardly ever enforced.

To this day, Cameroonians argue about the motivations for the Victoire raid. Court documents have since revealed that, a month earlier, a local official had reported concerns about "the existence of homes where young homosexuals and lesbians don't hesitate to indulge in their activities at night, in open air, in front of people including children younger than 15."[1] This report was forwarded to the head of the military police in the neighborhood, who ordered a raid on a house where several gay men lived. It's possible the police learned about the

Sunday gatherings at the Victoire while questioning the house's inhabitants.

Another theory centers on an alleged affair between a gay Cameroonian chef and his employer, a judge on the High Court of Justice. Either the judge's wife or the judge himself ordered the chef's arrest so he wouldn't be in a position to blackmail the family, the story goes, and the police came to the Victoire hoping to find him. This theory has not been proven, however, and the chef himself disavows any link to the raid, which would quickly come to represent a grim turning point for the position of sexual minorities in Cameroonian society.

During their first hours in custody, some of the men began paying bribes for their release. The asking price was as high as 250,000 CFA francs, or around $500, an enormous sum in Cameroon. Though he believed he could have called in favors to come up with the money, Lambert says he never seriously considered doing so; he would continue playing by the rules and cooperating with the police, as he had from the moment the raid began. After all, he reasoned, Cameroon's penal code criminalizes same-sex sexual acts, and all he had done was go out for drinks. None of the men, to his mind, was actually guilty of anything.

The first sign this might have been a miscalculation came the following day, when police instructed the remaining detainees to remove their shirts before marching them out into the police station's courtyard. There it became apparent that local authorities would use the case to try and send a larger message. Journalists from two broadcast stations had been summoned, and the cameras began rolling. While some of the journalists attempted to conduct interviews, it was clear they had already accepted police claims that the men were part of "a homosexual gang."

Didier, who had not disclosed his attraction to men to anyone outside of a small circle of friends, many of whom were rounded up at the Victoire along with him, recalls trying to cover his face as the cameramen approached. His efforts were in vain. His family would have no trouble spotting him later on the evening news.

Even for those who, like Lambert, were open with their families about their sexual orientations, the coverage jeopardized their reputations in the city at large. "We were pariahs," Lambert says. "We were the ones who were ruining the country. They called us every bad thing."

* * *

The decision to broadcast the men's arrest so publicly—to make a national scandal out of what would otherwise have been an unseemly but private affair—marked a profound shift for a culture that had previously made no space for discussions of alternative sexualities. This silence was exactly what had enabled the men, up until the day of the raid, to hide in plain view, settling into a social rhythm organized around the few bars where they could come together.

Lambert had been instrumental in building up this scene for Yaoundé's population of men who have sex with men, willing into existence something that, as far as he knew, had never before been attempted. A stocky man with a sloping forehead and charged, arresting eyes, Lambert seemed capable at any given moment of erupting in either laughter or anger. The fact that it was almost always the former explained why people were drawn to him. The fact that the latter was a constant possibility made them appreciate the laughter even more.

In 2000, he founded Cameroon's first gay and lesbian rights organization, the Association for Gays and Lesbians and Supporters, or AGALES. Unlike the advocacy groups of today, AGALES had no funding and little by way of programming. Its main achievement, according to Lambert and other AGALES members, was to provide a ready-made network for people eager to learn about the Victoire and the men's other meeting spots. These bars were not strictly gay bars, but Lambert and his friends viewed them as safe. If the more effeminate among them became too effusive in their greetings or demonstrative in their dancing, they risked a beating, perhaps, but that was the worst of it.

The mass arrests in May 2005 marked the first serious attack on this scene, signaling that gay men, and sexual minorities in general, had become subjects of interest to the police and other agents of the state.

The initial hostility Lambert and his fellow detainees encountered from the police was matched, if not exceeded, by court officials. During their first court appearance, several days after the raid, these officials made clear to the eleven men who remained in custody that they were already guilty in the eyes of the law. One prosecutor said homosexuality was unjustifiable because there were "more women than men" in Cameroon. She accused the suspects of driving women to prostitution and wrecking other people's marriages. She told them they would need to go to Europe if they wanted to continue being *pédés*. Then she ordered them jailed as they awaited trial.

And so, ten days after the raid, the men were escorted two-by-two, in chains, through the entrance of the city's central prison, known as Kondengui, a facility whose forbidding, earth-stained walls have long symbolized a criminal justice system that emphasizes cruelty and suffering over any kind of rehabilitation. Built in the 1960s, during the first decade of Cameroon's independence, Kondengui, like many prisons in the region, is poorly maintained and overcrowded, and has been this way for as long as anyone can remember. Three years before the Victoire raid, a local human rights group reported that there were 9,530 detainees housed there, despite the fact that it was built for 2,500 (US Department of State 2003).

Thanks to the media coverage their case had received, the men's reputations preceded them. When they came in view of the other prisoners, Didier says, "It was like we were the stars." The shouts of "Here come the *pédés*" and "Here come the women" caused Stéphane to break down in tears almost immediately. "It was a horror," he says. Didier remembers that the oldest of the Victoire detainees, a fifty-year-old clothing designer named Pascal, was singled out in taunts that reflected the widespread belief in Cameroon that gay men prey on young boys. "Look at the old guy. You don't have anything better to do?" the prisoners shouted. "You're spoiling everyone's children."

Because they totaled eleven—the same number as a side in a soccer match—the men were mockingly referred to as the "Indomitable Lions," the name of Cameroon's national team. The prisoners even gave the men positions; Didier recalls that he was referred to as the center midfielder, while Lambert, walking in front, was nicknamed "captain."

Following this welcome, officials began assigning the men to different sections of the prison. The men were presented with a choice. If they confessed to violating Article 347 bis, they would be kept in sections reserved for elite prisoners, including former government ministers who had run afoul of the law. These areas were less populated than the rest of the prison, and were vigilantly policed by guards.

If, on the other hand, they maintained their innocence, they would be sent to a section of the prison known, for its violence, as Kosovo. "Kosovo was the jungle. It was a bit like Soweto, like Vietnam," Didier says. "It really was a disaster." In Kosovo, cells were severely overcrowded and inmates, not guards, were appointed by prison officials to keep the peace. In exchange, they were given carte blanche to demand small payments for nearly every service; prisoners even had to pay to leave their cells and walk around.

To underscore the dangers the men might face there, prison officials displayed weapons, including knives, they said had been recovered from Kosovo inmates. Peter Kumche, director of Trauma Centre, an NGO based in Yaoundé that provides support to inmates at Kondengui, says such intimidatory tactics are standard practice. "Normally, they use very unorthodox methods to get a confession. They can beat you, they can use all kinds of methods—strategies that are unconventional," he says. "And so when you stand on your position and you refuse to confess, it is possible that they can think that you are very hardened, that you are hard-hearted, and that you are a very dangerous person."

It would be difficult, Kumche adds, to overstate the risks posed by incarceration in Kosovo. "Kosovo is a section of the prison which is reserved for hardened criminals," he says. "These are people whom the government thinks need to receive the worst treatment to compensate for the crime that has been committed."

Ultimately, eight of the eleven men heeded the prison officials' warnings and agreed to sign a confession so they could be housed in the more secure sections. The three who did not were Didier, Lambert and Alim Mongoche, a twenty-nine-year-old clothing designer from a Muslim family in Cameroon's Far North Region.

* * *

Lambert had never met Alim prior to their arrest. He was physically small, more timid than Lambert and Didier and, quite clearly, terrified, at times even trembling with fear. This made him an easy target. According to Lambert and lawyer Alice Nkom, who would eventually represent the group at trial, Alim was raped multiple times soon after they arrived at Kondengui, with other inmates sometimes using drugs to render him defenseless. "They would use pills, drugs, put tranquilizers in your food," Lambert later told the French documentary filmmaker Céline Metzger (2009). "After you ate, you'd feel tired and they'd drag you to their beds." When Lambert complained to prison authorities on Alim's behalf, they refused to step in and do anything. One time, when Alim tried to resist his attackers, they responded with a beating that left Alim in the infirmary for a week.

Violence touched the lives of the others, too. Lambert fought off a rape attempt one time in the bathroom. And Didier, though he was not attacked himself, says he became accustomed to witnessing fights that involved large numbers of prisoners, some of whom had access to weapons including razor blades and machetes. With inmates policing Kosovo themselves, these fights were rarely broken up. Didier estimates that he witnessed twenty deaths, as well as a number of gruesome injuries; once, he watched as a prisoner had his face cut open and his eye stabbed out. Kosovo, Didier says, was governed by "the law of the strongest."

Despite these incidents, Didier sympathized with his fellow inmates, many of whom he suspected were driven to violence because of the conditions in Kondengui. His own cell had sixty-three inmates assigned to it, while Lambert's had forty-five for just eighteen bunks. The constant bribe requests forced prisoners to come up with money either from visitors or by performing cleaning and maintenance tasks, and fights could break out over as little as 5 CFA francs—not even a penny. "The prisoners were working," Didier says. "They woke up at 5 a.m. and organized themselves so they didn't waste the day."

They also had to find ways to supplement their diets. The prison-issued meals, which came once a day, were simply not enough to live on. Two days a week, Lambert says, inmates received a spoonful of "rice soup" with peanut sauce poured into their cupped hands. The rest of the time they were offered boiled corn. Lambert was luckier than most: His mother owned a restaurant in Yaoundé, and she regularly came by with fish and other meals. Even so, his weight fell and his health faltered.

Those who couldn't hustle for money or a place to sleep—because they were too old, say, or too ill—were slowly worn down by the place. Didier remembers watching two men in their sixties who slept on a plastic tarp in an open courtyard each night, even when rain had turned the red earth to mud. "They weren't even young men, with the strength to bear certain things," he says. "They were old men. Why did the government need to put them in jail? Does the government not understand that they are old? I asked myself this question, and I understood then that the law is the law. It strikes everyone."

* * *

Even in this setting, the Victoire detainees settled into something of a routine, making the most of their situation while awaiting word on how long it might last. It would be months before they received a trial date.

Didier took his incarceration as an opportunity for self-reflection; Kondengui, he says, was a kind of personal university. "I didn't understand why I was living in disorder," he says, noting that he had been especially devastated by his inability to find anyone to help him cobble together $500 so he could bribe his way to freedom when the men were first arrested. After he was sent to Kondengui, his sister was the only member of his family who came to visit him and bring him money.

He quickly made friends in Kosovo, and began attending a prayer group. He also began studying under an inmate who worked as a professional carpenter, learning skills that would help him rebuild his life upon his release.

Stéphane had a rougher transition. Fearing the violence of Kosovo, he had chosen to confess to violating Article 347 bis in exchange for a placement in Quartier 1, where he was housed next to former high-ranking government officials. Explaining his rationale, he says, "I was very effeminate, very cute, with long hair. If the people in Kosovo had seen me, maybe they would've raped me."

He soon grew frustrated, however, with the restrictions of Quartier 1, where actual prison guards were posted and rules against drinking and smoking were strictly enforced. The break from his life outside was too much to bear, and he soon found himself sneaking off to Kosovo. "Everybody was surprised," he says. "They said, 'Why would you want to go there?' I said, 'No, I feel better there. I can drink, I can smoke, it's clandestine.'"

Though he faced the constant threat of attack, he found he could use his sexuality to his advantage. The catcalling began as soon he headed to the shower in the morning, but this attention—he refers to it today as "appreciation"—gave him a degree of power. "I was the mother hen," he says. Guards and inmates alike would approach him for sex, and he learned how to decline without really declining. "I'd say, 'Yes, sure, tomorrow.'" In the meantime, these men were willing to grant Stéphane favors; the inmates-turned-guards in Kosovo, for instance, would allow him and his friends to enter the main courtyard without paying the usual fee. "I exercised control with my strength of character," Stéphane says. "I adapted fast. At the beginning, I was a bit depressed, but then I said to myself, 'You need to not be depressed. Carry your head high.'"

Lambert, for his part, had a quieter existence. Because his cell was so overcrowded, he had to spend his nights on the floor. But he eventually struck up a friendship with one of the prisoners who had bunk access, and who allowed Lambert to use his bunk during the day. Each morning, then, after rising before dawn to bathe, Lambert came back to the cell and caught up on the sleep he'd missed the night before.

He discovered he could visit the prison library two times per week and check out books. Having stopped his education in middle school, Lambert had never been a regular reader. But he soon began passing his free time engrossed in the prison's ragtag collection of encyclopedias, as well as the occasional novel. He loved in particular *Perfume: The Story of a Murderer*, by the German writer Patrick Suskind, in which the protagonist, Jean-Baptiste Grenouille, an orphan who was born with a perfect sense of smell, kills young women to capture their scents. Though he struggled to remember the novel's title, more than ten years later he could still recount the details of its plot, including the ending, when Grenouille, in the middle of a crowd in Paris, douses himself in a perfume so alluring it compels those around him to tear him to pieces—an act they perform "out of love." It was, Lambert says, a "very beautiful story."

Lambert also looked after his fellow Victoire detainees as best he could, organizing meetings to make sure they were safe and that they had something to eat. "This was a milieu where you saw the limits of men," Didier says. "People didn't share. Lambert, he didn't have a lot, but he was very organized, and he made sure we had the means to eat, to have a little meal each night." Didier recalls how Lambert managed to perform other small favors; one time, for example, he found Didier a pen, which Didier needed for the prayer group he had enrolled in.

Several weeks after their arrival at Kondengui, Lambert himself put pen to paper on the men's behalf. Sitting on his borrowed bunk, he wrote a letter detailing what had happened to them: the raid at the Victoire, their arrest, the verbal abuse from police and court officials, their transfer to Kondengui and the unforgiving conditions they encountered there. He was able to slip the letter to a visiting friend, and instructed this friend to post its contents online.

It was a move driven, more than anything else, by a desire to ward off feelings of helplessness, to assert some semblance of control over a bewildering, destabilizing situation. So much was still unclear at that point. Lambert didn't know how long he and his fellow detainees would continue to receive outside support from family and friends, or how long they could stay healthy in Kondengui. Officials could not give them any information on whether and when their case might go to trial.

Similarly, Lambert had no way of knowing the extent to which writing this letter, more than any other decision he made during the men's ordeal, would shape their remaining time behind bars, as well as everything that came after.

2

Do no harm

Charles Gueboguo was as surprised as anyone to learn about the Victoire raid. A Cameroonian sociologist, Gueboguo had familiarized himself with the lives of gay men in Cameroon's two main cities, Yaoundé and Douala, while conducting the research that would form the basis of his first book, *La question homosexuelle en Afrique: le cas du Cameroun*, published in 2006. He had seen for himself the freedoms gay men in the country enjoyed, and how the wider society generally refrained from acknowledging, at least publicly, the world Lambert and his friends had created. Not once in the course of this work had Gueboguo heard of anything approaching the scale of the crackdown that ensnared Lambert and the other ten men. Though activists would later become more diligent about documenting arrests and other attempts to enforce Article 347 bis, Cameroon's penal code provision criminalizing same-sex

sexual acts, up until 2005 such incidents had been so rare as
to barely register beyond those immediately affected.

The man who brought the raid to Gueboguo's attention was Joel Nana, a Cameroonian gay rights activist and a
member of AGALES, the organization for gays and lesbians
that Lambert had founded in 2000. After the letter Lambert
wrote from prison began to circulate, Nana had been in
contact with Alice Nkom, the lawyer, and the two of them
had begun discussing how best to respond. The unprecedented nature of the case meant that everyone, activists
included, was acting blindly, without the benefit of protocol.

Nkom was something of a pathbreaker long before she
began defending Cameroonian sexual minorities against
legal persecution. In 1969, she had become the first
woman admitted to the Cameroonian bar, and she built
up a practice representing women victims of sexual and
domestic violence as well as political prisoners detained
under Cameroon's founding president, Ahmadou Ahidjo.

As she describes it, her interest in gay rights, and specifically in trying to overturn Article 347 bis, can be traced
back to an incident that took place two years before the
Victoire raid. One day, in early 2003, she received visitors
to her Douala office, French tourists who had mutual
friends and had stopped by to say hello. "I understood
immediately that they were more than friends, and that this
happiness could be threatened if the others recognized that
they were more than friends," she says. "So I wondered if
I needed to let them know that Cameroon is a country

that penalizes homosexuality." Eventually, in conversation with one of the men, she explained the legal situation. "I saw his face change, because he didn't know," she says. "He realized that they weren't in France, and that, in the world, all countries aren't like France. That made me feel very bad. I felt guilty, because I didn't have the right to stop people from being happy."

She began thinking that, because of what she'd said, perhaps the men wouldn't come back to Cameroon, and that perhaps gay Cameroonians living in Europe and elsewhere might also choose to stay abroad. That single exchange, then, and the anxiety it sparked in her mind about Cameroon's place in the world, prompted her to consider creating an organization that could bring about legal reform.

Nkom had no prior experience with gay rights activism, nor had she heard of AGALES, Lambert's group. But she quickly learned that her position as a heterosexual woman, someone who was unlikely to be accused of violating the law she was trying to change, enabled her to take bold stands in her interactions with the state. This began with her move to register her organization, which she named the Association for the Defense of the Rights of Homosexuals, or ADEFHO, with authorities in Douala.

Lambert had never considered registering AGALES, fearing the official scrutiny such a move would bring. Even today, those LGBT organizations that are formally registered generally avoid featuring words like "gay," "homosexual" or "lesbian" in their names, instead emphasizing, in many cases, their work promoting testing and treatment for HIV/AIDS. Nkom had no such reservations. She knew she was being provocative; that was precisely the point. During a contentious meeting with the local prefect, the official responsible for approving her registration request, Nkom argued that the constitution's language about the protection of minorities applied to sexual minorities as well, and that this trumped any specific law that might be used against them. In the end, Nkom got her way. ADEFHO was officially recognized by the state in 2003, a milestone for the work that would eventually bring her awards and, at least in LGBT activist circles, no small amount of fame.

In the early days, though, there was little she could do to move that work along. Because arrests were rare—so rare, in fact, that Nkom had never heard of any—there were no cases she could bring to challenge Article 347 bis in court. The Victoire raid changed that. "I read that in the newspaper, and I thought, 'OK,'" she says, smiling and rubbing the palms of her hands together. "ADEFHO can now begin its work."

* * *

ADEFHO was not the only organization for which the Victoire raid would serve as a kind of training exercise. After learning of the arrests, Nana and Gueboguo attended a conference on LGBT issues in Marseilles, France, during which they discussed the situation in Yaoundé and decided that more international attention would be helpful.

Shortly thereafter, they came into contact with the New York-based International Gay and Lesbian Human Rights Commission, or IGLHRC, which is often described as the first organization to advocate for LGBT rights worldwide.[1]

Cary Alan Johnson, IGLHRC's Africa coordinator at the time, recalls that he immediately recognized the potential value of the case. For one thing, it fit squarely within the human rights framework that had guided IGLHRC's work since its founding in 1990. In *Transnational LGBT Activism: Working for Sexual Rights Worldwide*, a book published in 2014 that traces the history of IGLHRC, Ryan R. Thoreson describes how the organization evolved over time in response to pressure, both internal and external, to prioritize cultural, political and socio-economic rights. But Johnson says that in 2005 IGLHRC was still focused on human rights abuses such as violence and arbitrary arrests perpetrated by state actors. This approach matched Johnson's own experience and expertise. "I come from a very sort of traditional human rights background—Amnesty International, prisoner of conscience," he says. "Arbitrary detentions is my bread and butter." Describing his reaction to news of the Victoire raid, he recalled thinking, "'Now we're talking. I know what to do with a case like that.'"

As a general rule, that may have been true. But in many respects, by Johnson's own admission, IGLHRC didn't really know what to do with the case of the Victoire raid. "First of all, I had never been to Cameroon, and we didn't have any Africans on our staff at the time, and certainly no Cameroonians," he says. "And we had a very basic knowledge of where the pressure points were and how to use the UN system at that point. The movement globally is much more mature now than it was then. So, you know, we were kind of putting it together as we went along, and trying very hard to do no harm."

IGLHRC first attempted to identify on-the-ground organizations that could make sure any money sent from abroad would reach the men behind bars. It eventually convinced Trauma Centre, the Yaoundé-based group run by Peter Kumche, to come to the men's aid. As Kumche recalls, Trauma Centre's decision to get involved was not taken lightly, and involved extensive deliberations by its board of directors. "The board was reluctant because LGBT in Cameroon is penalized by the law," Kumche says. "And so once you start working for LGBT, you are considered as working against the law." In the end, the board came around to the argument that, regardless of their sexual orientations, the men had been victims of torture in Kondengui and, for that reason, were deserving of assistance.

Trauma Centre staff began visiting Lambert and the others in prison while also trying to identify a lawyer who would take up their case. While it was easy enough for Kumche to get the men money and food, finding legal representation proved frustrating. The first team that offered to help simply encouraged the men to bribe their way out of trouble, something Lambert refused to do, just as he had back at the police station when they were first taken into custody. Johnson was at a loss as to how to find someone who would be interested in trying the case on the merits.

Then Alice, based in Douala, came on IGLHRC's radar, seemingly out of nowhere. "All of a sudden there's this Alice. I don't know who she is, but she's big, she's got a big presence," Johnson says. "Who is she? What does she want exactly? Can we trust her? There was some concern at first, but we didn't have too many friends, so at the same time there was this feeling of, 'Good.'" Nkom began submitting filings on the men's behalf, and she and the other activists continued to document their treatment in Kondengui.

This treatment had not improved; if anything, it was getting worse. In September 2005, prison offi-cials ordered that Lambert and the other detainees be subjected to forced anal exams, a pseudoscientific form of torture used in some countries to "prove" that an indi-vidual has engaged in anal sex. As IGLHRC noted in a statement, the exams, which had previously been used in countries including Egypt, Romania and Zimbabwe, "rely on the false idea that anal sex leaves lasting lesions or tears around the anus. Often involving insertions of instru-ments into the anus, they are profoundly humiliating to those forced to undergo them" (IGLHRC 2005). In an angry filing, Nkom noted that this order was made several months after the men had arrived at Kondengui, where some of them, notably Alim, had been subjected to sexual assault. Therefore, even if the exams were capable of demonstrating same-sex sexual activity—which they are not—such results would just as likely have reflected the abuse they'd endured behind bars than any sex they'd been having before their arrival.

As it happened, doctors refused to carry out the procedure. Yet the fact that the exams were ordered at all helped sustain international interest in the case, especially among those unfamiliar with what life is like for sexual minorities living under governments that actively persecute them. Johnson, who had begun referring to Lambert and his fellow detainees as the "Yaoundé 11," remembers that interest in their story seemed practically limitless. For many outsiders, the mere fact of the men's detention was eye-opening, and deeply troubling. "People found it astounding that you could really be arrested for simply being in a public space, and so I think it had a lot of resonance," Johnson says.

Other organizations followed IGLHRC's lead and took up the cause of the "Yaoundé 11," including Amnesty International-France and the International Lesbian and Gay Association. The interest from global activists soon reached a level of intensity that startled everyone, especially Cameroonian officials. As letters of support for the men flooded in from around the world, Lambert remembers that two prosecutors came to question him. The few previous cases brought under Article 347 bis had elicited no reaction, and they wanted to know why this one was different. "They wanted to know why, with me, the entire world was interested in Cameroon," Lambert says. "They even asked me, 'Do you work in a secret service?'"

* * *

The Cameroonian prosecutors were onto something. This type of global scrutiny of how African countries treated sexual minorities was indeed a new phenomenon, one made possible by the rapid global proliferation of LGBT-focused advocacy organizations in the years leading up to the Victoire raid. As Thoreson (2014) notes in his book, the vast majority—nearly 90 percent—of international LGBT groups and programs date back no earlier than 1990, the year IGLHRC was founded.

Broadly speaking, though, foreigner-led interventions in the lives of sexual minorities in Africa are not new at all. Rather, they align with a centuries-old tradition of outsiders wielding disproportionate influence over the ways sexual minorities on the continent are perceived and treated. The difference lies in what's motivating these interventions, and what they're intended to achieve. Today, many interventions—though not all of them, by any means—fit the general mold of IGLHRC in Cameroon: They represent well-meaning, if at times naive, attempts to bring rights and protections widely enjoyed in places like the United States and Western Europe to a continent that has acquired a reputation, however overstated, for homophobia. Throughout the eighteenth, nineteenth and much of the twentieth centuries, by contrast, outsiders' interventions were decidedly less benevolent.

During this period, the small army of European researchers who traveled to Africa, ostensibly in hopes of developing a genuine understanding of how life was lived there, demonstrated a seemingly unshakable faith in a fundamentally misguided notion: that alternative sexualities were somehow "un-African." In the preface to their 1998 book *Boy Wives and Female Husbands: Studies in African Sexualities*, Stephen O. Murray and Will Roscoe describe several of the factors that gave rise to this belief. And in his 2008 book *Heterosexual Africa? The History of an Idea from the Age of Exploration to the Age of AIDS*, Marc Epprecht explains how it has persisted and evolved.

Many of these foreigners had, even before embarking on their journeys, bought into claims that Africans lived in a kind of a pre-civilized state. "For Europeans, black Africans—of all the native peoples in the world—most epitomized 'primitive man,'" Murray and Roscoe write. "Since primitive man was supposed to be close to nature, ruled by instinct, and culturally unsophisticated, he had to be heterosexual, his sexual energies and outlets devoted exclusively to their 'natural' purpose: biological reproduction."

The idea that Africans were primitive subjects in need of civilizing underpinned the entire colonial project. It served an additional purpose in the context of European morality debates over sexuality. Because they were seen as untainted by decadent social and sexual practices on display in London and elsewhere in Europe, Africans provided a "noble savage" counterpoint to everything that was wrong back home. Murray and Roscoe (1998) note that this thinking appeared in print as far back as the late eighteenth century, when Edward Gibbon published his *History of the Decline and Fall of the Roman Empire*. Referring to homosexuality, Gibbon writes, "I believe, and hope, that the negroes, in their own country, were exempt from this moral pestilence."

Other explanations for why evidence of alternative sexualities went largely unmentioned in most colonial-era writings had to do with the specific arrangements that made this work possible. Many researchers were employed by colonial governments directly, meaning they had reason to avoid discussing things that made those governments look bad, including the ways colonial systems—for instance, all-male mining camps—facilitated same-sex sexual acts. Researchers' findings were also likely shaped by fears of offending a readership in Europe that would potentially have been scandalized by any mention of homosexuality whatsoever.

The result of all this is a body of work that, as Epprecht (2008) writes, "expresses an opinion of what African sexuality should be like, rather than what it really is." That opinion, he writes, can be summed up as follows: that Africans "are virtually unique in the world in the absence of, ignorance about, or intolerance toward exceptions to the heterosexual norm."

Of course, same-sex sexual practices did exist in Africa. While they were often blamed on the influence of inter-lopers, including Arab traders active on the East African coast, some researchers saw them instead as natural. Writing in 1921, the German ethnographer Gunther Tessman noted that same-sex sexual relations among boys from Cameroon's Bafia group were so common as to be considered a "national custom." Tessman writes: "Since the boys—as they say—don't hesitate to have intercourse with their fellows by day at home, it sometimes happens that the father will chance upon them. But he only laughs over it, and in no way punishes his boy." The boys were expected to stop once they were old enough to have sex with girls and start families of their own, but this didn't always happen. Boys, Tessman wrote, were notorious for having "neither understanding nor shame," and older men who wished to sleep with them could "readily console them by saying, 'We are having fun, playing a game'" (in Murray and Roscoe 1998).

Like the researchers who ignored such behavior, Tessman may have had his own agenda. He has been described as a "repressed homosexual," and his work was probably shaped by discussions unfolding back home in Germany. His 1921 assertion that same-sex sexual activity in Cameroon shows that "homosexual desires are firmly established in human nature" echoes a point stressed at the time by those campaigning to change Germany's law banning homosexuality.

His findings, though, are buttressed by more recent research detailing examples of African sexualities as diverse as the continent itself. To cite just a few: In northern Nigeria, Rudolf P. Gaudio has described the role of *yan daudu*, men "who are unabashedly open in their adoption of womanlike behaviors" and who play the role of "wives" in relationships with more discreet "husbands." In South Africa, Graeme Reid (2013) has written about how gender expression shapes sexual encounters between men in small towns, where so-called "ladies" who wear makeup and women's clothing pursue relationships with gender-conforming "gents." And in Lesotho, Judith Gay (1985) has documented romantic relationships in all-female boarding schools featuring dominant "Mummies" and deferential "Babies." Though they generally don't conform to egalitarian same-sex relationship models privileged in the United States and Europe, such cases show that in Africa, as elsewhere, sex is not restricted to couplings of men and women.

It is tempting to think about how perceptions of sexual minorities in Africa might be different today had early researchers simply followed the evidence available to them. One intriguing case is that of E.E. Evans-Pritchard, an English anthropologist acclaimed for his 1937 study *Witchcraft, Oracles and Magic Among the Zande*. The book makes no mention of homosexuality, but that doesn't mean Evans-Pritchard hadn't heard about it. To the contrary, his informants in northern Congo described relationships between warriors and young boys; the older men would even present a "bride price" to boys' families. They also reported relationships involving women who "have sexual intercourse between them with sweet potatoes carved in the shape of a circumcised penis, with carved manioc, and also with bananas."

Evans-Prichard's findings might have undermined claims that alternative sexualities were inherently foreign to African populations. But he withheld them for many years, writing about them for the first time more than a decade after his original study was published. They did not reach a wide audience until 1970, just a few years before he died and long after narratives of African sexualities had been warped by colonial-era blinders.

* * *

These days, it has become a truism among African LGBT activists that, contrary to popular opinion, homosexuality is not a Western import. Rather, they say, homophobia is.

On one level, these activists are referring specifically to the history of anti-gay legislation on the continent. More than two-thirds of African countries have laws criminalizing same-sex sexual conduct between consenting adults. While some of these laws, including Cameroon's Article 347 bis, were drafted after independence, the wording of many of the others leaves little mystery as to their origins. Uganda, a former British protectorate, and Kenya, a former British colony, are among the countries that ban "carnal knowledge against the order of nature"—language that closely resembles an old clause under English common law.

Beyond legislation, these activists are also describing how colonial-era beliefs concerning alternative sexualities—in particular, that they violate so-called African traditions—were taken up by African scholars, politicians and religious leaders. In many cases, this process involved direct interactions with institutions of the colonizing power that, at the very least, reinforced these Africans' views of how sexuality on the continent was lived. Before he became Kenya's founding president, for example, Jomo Kenyatta trained to become an anthropologist at the London School of Economics. Epprecht (2008) notes that in a study of his Kikuyu ethnic group published in 1939, Kenyatta dismisses homosexuality as an "unnecessary" practice. "Any form of sexual intercourse other than the natural form, between men and women acting in a normal way, is out of the question," Kenyatta writes. "It is considered taboo even to have sexual intercourse with a woman in any position except the regular one, face to face."

Yet despite the existence of anti-gay laws and the pervasive nature of homophobic thinking among the African intelligentsia, the issue of homosexuality was of marginal concern in the first decades after independence. Enforcement of anti-gay laws in most countries ranged from patchy to non-existent, and debates over homosexuality had little political salience. This remained the case up until the 1990s, when two countries in southern Africa adopted starkly different stances on the issue.

Following the toppling of South Africa's apartheid regime in 1990, the country's new leadership proved itself to be strikingly progressive in its treatment of sexual minorities. The new constitution, ratified in 1996, was the first in the world to ban discrimination based on sexual orientation, paving the way for the adoption of same-sex marriage a decade later. Explanations of what gave rise to these freedoms point to the close involvement of gay and lesbian activists in the fight against apartheid as well as widespread hostility—after the downfall of a system built on racism—to the exclusion of any group, for any reason.

Neighboring Zimbabwe went in the opposite direction, though this wouldn't have been easy to predict. When Robert Mugabe first came to power in 1980, Zimbabwe was a refuge for South Africans fleeing the anti-gay apartheid regime. The capital, Harare, boasted a lively gay scene as well as one of the continent's first formal associations for sexual minorities: Gays and Lesbians of Zimbabwe, or GALZ, founded in 1989. This tolerance vanished abruptly, however, in the 1990s. Epprecht (2008) has convincingly framed this shift as part of Mugabe's more sweeping denunciation of the West in response to donor-imposed structural adjustment policies that dented Zimbabwe's economy and threatened Mugabe's legitimacy. Sexual minorities, tainted by "Western" social mores, were an effective stand-in for the forces Mugabe believed were driving his government, and the country, to ruin. In one of the earliest versions of his many anti-gay jeremiads, on August 1, 1995, Mugabe described homosexuality as "against the laws of nature and the morals of religious beliefs espoused by our society." Before long he would be infamous for denouncing gay people as "worse than dogs and pigs."

A few other African leaders followed Mugabe's lead. But such outbursts were high-profile exceptions to the rule that governed the lives of Lambert and most other sexual minorities who came of age before the 2000s: Because homosexuality was viewed as a problem primarily afflicting other societies in other parts of the world, neither the state nor the general population cared to discuss it, let alone police it.

Lambert and the rest of the Yaoundé 11 had no way of knowing it at the time, but the Victoire raid would mark the beginning of the end of this relatively laissez-faire approach in Cameroon. Within less than a decade, the government of President Paul Biya would develop a global reputation for being particularly anti-gay, having carried out dozens of arrests and prosecutions, many of which would result in convictions. Given that the organizations tracking these cases have a presence only in Douala and Yaoundé and rely on word-of-mouth in collecting data, it is widely suspected that their tallies reflect only a portion of all arrests taking place.

The deteriorating climate for sexual minorities led to ramped-up engagement on the part of international organizations like IGLHRC. But as these organizations would learn in Cameroon and elsewhere, deciding to become an ally is only the first step toward acting in sexual minorities' best interests. Along the way, a host of pitfalls can cause even the most well-intentioned outsiders to violate their wish, as articulated by IGLHRC's Johnson, to "do no harm."

Yet throughout 2005, as the mobilization inspired by Lambert's prison letter gathered momentum, the events that would highlight these pitfalls in the Cameroonian context were still some months in the future. In the meantime, Lambert enthusiastically took meetings with Nkom, Kumche and others whose involvement was being funded by outside money, confident that the widespread concern inspired by their case would result in their freedom.

Stéphane and the other detainees remember that while Lambert's emergence as the group's de facto public representative caused some resentment at first, this faded as it became clear he was best-suited for the job. Even with his limited education, he spoke effectively on their behalf. "He expressed himself the best and could make people understand," Gueboguo says. "The others didn't have a great education, so Lambert became like a spokesman for them."

Didier describes the role Lambert played for the group as that of an "older brother." It was a role that had largely gone unfilled during Lambert's own youth, when he had been left to figure out how to build a life as a gay man in Cameroon largely on his own.

3

More fear
than joy

Lambert was born in Yaoundé's Central Hospital in August 1974, the youngest of eight children, two boys and six girls. He spent the first years of his life in a house on a hill behind a Catholic church. The house was cramped, but the family's land was extensive enough to accommodate the children. It sloped down at the back, granting expansive views of the city between mango trees, flowers and the fanned-out palms of the occasional *arbre du voyageur*.

Lambert's father rode his Vespa each morning to the presidential palace, where he worked in catering during the administration of President Ahmadou Ahidjo. When Lambert was a toddler, his father accepted his first overseas posting to do similar work at the Cameroonian Embassy in Brazzaville, the capital of the Republic of Congo,

Cameroon's neighbor to the south. Lambert's parents hoped the assignment would lead to postings in other countries and, one day, maybe even at the embassy in Paris.

The family all moved together, and the kids adjusted as well as could be expected to their new home and new schools. For the parents, however, the transition was more difficult. Even four decades later, it pains Lambert to speak at much length about the breakdown of their marriage, and he was so young when it happened that he can't say with any confidence what the source of their problems was. What he does remember is the loud, violent beatings his mother endured at the hands of his father, and how his father would sometimes force his mother to sleep outside in the courtyard of their property. Lambert would occasionally go outside to sleep with her, huddling close to her as she nursed her bruises.

Eventually, the ambassador got wind of the situation, which was attracting unwanted attention from neighbors, and dreams of a Paris posting were scuttled. The family was sent back to Cameroon, and Lambert's mother, who at the time worked as a fish vendor and was capable of supporting herself, moved out.

Her departure affected Lambert most of all, according to his brothers and sisters. Once brash and confident, often teasing his older siblings, he became lost and withdrawn. "He was the youngest, and the youngest children often know that they can antagonize the older ones, because they are under the protection of their parents," recalls

Lambert's older brother, Jules. But with his mother gone, and his father, who served in the role of neighborhood chief, often away adjudicating disputes involving other families, Lambert lost this layer of protection and security.

His sense of vulnerability and isolation was compounded by his sexuality. From an early age, this set him apart for the rest of his siblings, occasionally resulting in minor scandals. One day, when he was thirteen or so, he was playing with a neighbor boy on the family compound in Yaoundé, and the two began to experiment with anal sex. The boy, Blaise, experienced anal bleeding, and Lambert, panicking at the injury, ran away to hide. Later that day, Blaise's mother, enraged, came to confront Lambert's family and tell them what had happened, becoming the first person to clue them into the notion that their son might be different.

Initially, Lambert's family dismissed the behavior as a phase. Though such incidents were not often discussed openly, same-sex sexual experimentation among children has long been documented in Cameroon. Writing a century ago, Gunther Tessman, the German ethnographer, described games among the Pangwe and Bafia tribes such as "hen-and-hawk," a form of hide-and-seek for boys "that culminates with the hawk 'mounting' the hen" (in Murray and Roscoe 1998). Lambert himself recalls playing similar games with classmates as a young student, both in Brazzaville and Yaoundé.

But the fact that Lambert's sexual experimentation with other boys continued through adolescence eventually became a source of tension, with his older siblings beating him and calling him *pédé*. What had initially been seen as innocent child's play became a problem no one knew how to solve.

At least in his younger years, though, Lambert's sexuality was more fluid than his siblings' taunts suggested. His schoolyard experimentation involved girls as much as boys, and he dated and slept with girls as a teenager, even having a brief fling with one of Jules' girlfriends, the source of a bitter feud that left the brothers so angry they hardly spoke for years.

This ambiguity may have helped preserve Lambert's position in the family. Despite the rough treatment at the hands of his siblings, he was never thrown out of the house. Instead, when he did leave, at age twenty-one, he did so on his own terms. "It's true that the situation wasn't ideal, but it was my choice to leave," he says. "They didn't chase me." Lambert's father placed a lock on Lambert's childhood bedroom, preserving his things as he'd left them in case he ever chose to return.

* * *

The turmoil within Lambert's family, culminating in his mother's departure, prompted Lambert and his siblings to reassess nearly every aspect of their lives, including their relationship to the authority figures with which they'd been raised. For most of them, this process involved an interrogation of their views on religion.

Abandoning their previous adherence to their father's Catholicism, the children set about shaping their own spiritual lives. Jules, Lambert's brother, became enamored of the Christian evangelical churches that have seen staggering growth in much of sub-Saharan Africa in recent decades. Lambert sampled a number of these churches himself— "searching," he remembers, "for God, or the truth."

Ultimately, though, he followed the lead of another sibling, one of his sisters, and began worshipping with the Jehovah's Witnesses. He quickly came to believe he had found a home with them. Jobless, and with little interest in continuing his studies, he had no shortage of free time. Before long, he was walking the streets of his neighborhood selling copies of *The Watchtower*, the Jehovah's Witnesses' monthly magazine, for 100 CFA francs, or less than a quarter.

It was on one of these routes that Lambert met the man who would give his life new purpose and direction, though the truth this man had to offer could not be found in any Bible. Paul Kamden, then in his thirties, was at the forefront of Cameroon's embrace of computer technology, familiarizing himself with Microsoft Windows and other programs before they came into wide use. In the 1990s, he opened one of Yaoundé's first cybercafés and began teaching classes on how to use the internet.

Paul almost immediately took a liking to the unassuming teenager who would periodically drop by his office peddling *The Watchtower*. The boy's spiritual devotion, he says, was in those days visible even to casual passersby. He recalls, for example, watching one day as Lambert tried to talk a man out of smoking a cigarette—an act that Jehovah's Witnesses believe shows disrespect for the gift of life. "I felt the love of God in him," Paul says.

Paul was not especially religious, and he had little use for *The Watchtower*. But he grew protective of Lambert and decided to begin teaching the boy what he knew about computers. He permitted Lambert to sit in on classes for free, hoping the new skills would help him conquer his apparent timidity. "If you posed a question, even if he knew the answer, he didn't easily raise his hand," Paul says. "It's as if he was afraid."

Lambert's outward shyness masked a burning interest in the new machines and their potential. "It was the work of the future," Lambert says. "Before long, if you didn't know how to do it, you would be considered illiterate." He decided he would try to turn this interest into a career. After finishing his training with Paul, Lambert took a job at a different cybercafé in Yaoundé's upscale, expat-friendly Bastos neighborhood in the north of the city.

One of his main tasks at this new job was to type messages written longhand by customers who didn't have computers of their own. A surprising number of those who frequented the cybercafé, he discovered, were gay Cameroonian men perusing profiles on *sites de rencontre*, or matchmaking sites, based in Europe. These men were searching for foreign lovers keen on visiting Africa or, better yet, facilitating their travel to Europe, which in their minds was a gay man's paradise. Stéphane, who would later be rounded up along with Lambert in the Victoire raid, remembers that, in those days, a trip to the cybercafé was one of the closest things many gay men had to a night out. An hour online would cost 2,500 CFA francs, or about $5, and groups of men would pool their money and divvy up the time. "It was very expensive at the time, but we didn't have a choice," Stéphane says. "Everyone wanted to chat with a white. Everyone wanted to find a white who could help him leave Cameroon. They'd say, '*Voilà*, I'm going to find a white who will change my life.'"

These were not unreasonable fantasies. Plenty of gay men from countries such as France and Belgium were interested in pursuing relationships with Africans. They would fly down, as they still do, for extended stays, and some would even succeed in procuring visas for their African partners to travel home with them. Lambert watched several friends leave Cameroon this way. At first, he had no interest in setting up a matchmaking profile for himself, but a friend eventually managed to convince him that he was missing out. "He said to me, 'You work for others, they get to travel and all of that. You need to also work for yourself!'"

For the first few months, his profile was largely dormant. Then, in late 2000, Lambert struck up an online relationship with a European of his own.

* * *

Gérard reached out to Lambert first, sending a one-line message a few weeks before Christmas: "What are you doing here?"

Lambert grew anxious, thinking it was perhaps a disapproving relative. "But after reflecting, I thought, 'He is on the same site.' So I responded, 'The same thing as you.'"

Gérard introduced himself as a French academic who lived on Réunion Island, in the Indian Ocean. For years, he said, he had conducted fieldwork in Madagascar, but he was planning to retire so he could do more leisure travel.

In one of his first messages, hard copies of which Lambert keeps in a folder to this day, Gérard disclosed, with an air of apology, that he was older—fifty-five, he said—and that he was white. Lambert said this didn't bother him. In fact, he said, he had no problem with white people, and he claimed he preferred to date older men "because they have something to give me." He clarified the point: "When you are with young people, you pass your time drinking, gossiping about men and women," he said. "When you speak with older people you speak of ideas."

Gérard homed in on Lambert's interest in technology, and they traded what, to a third party, read like dry, clinical notes about internet speeds and computer specs. Lambert, though, was intrigued, and he became even more eager to develop the relationship when Gérard offered to bring him software from abroad.

By that point, Gérard had already decided he would travel to Cameroon the next month. Things were moving far more quickly than they typically did with such relationships, something Lambert attributed to "the ease of our exchanges, our dialogue." They had swapped headshots and spoken once or twice by phone. Gérard marveled at the photos and the sound of Lambert's "hot voice," and had taken to referring to Lambert as "*mon gentil black*." He disclosed that he was especially attracted to black men, something Lambert understood to be fairly common, given the messages he and his friends received. Gérard bought his ticket, and the two men began counting the days until they could meet in person.

Yet from the first moments of Gérard's arrival, their courtship grew more complicated. As it turned out, Gérard had also been chatting with another Cameroonian, and this man, like Lambert, showed up to greet him at the airport in Yaoundé, along with a small entourage. Gérard left the airport with this group. After long days of anticipation, then, Lambert had to settle for brief hello before beginning the ride back to Yaoundé alone, in a separate taxi.

In the days that followed, Lambert found it difficult to get any time at all with Gérard. The other Cameroonian had assumed the role of Gérard's protector, and warned him of the possibility that Lambert was an *arnaqueur*, or swindler. In reality, the opposite was true, as Lambert learned when he and Gérard were finally able to meet. As they went around the city, visiting crafts markets and roadside food stands, Gérard noticed that Lambert was paying for everything, and began asking him about the cost of taxis and other services. He realized that the Cameroonian who'd been hosting him—and who had been using Gérard's money to pay for whatever they needed—was severely inflating the cost of everything from having a shirt ironed to spending an hour in a cybercafé. Furious, Gérard decided that he would rather stay with Lambert, packed his bags and left.

Lambert and Gérard spent their first full day together having a lunch of grilled fish and red wine with Lambert's family. Then they found a new hotel for Gérard, one sufficiently far from the Cameroonian who had fleeced him and was now sending him death threats via text message. That first night, Lambert stayed over, thinking they would finally be able to sleep together. But while they tried to have sex, Lambert couldn't maintain an erection. "Gérard understood that, sexually, he didn't work for me," Lambert says.

They spent the night in the same bed anyway, and the next day Lambert started showing Gérard his favorite bars. He also introduced him to other gay men, including several who were more than happy to sleep with a wealthy French visitor. Yet even as Gérard found other men to sleep with, he remained closest to Lambert. More often than not during his stay, Lambert spent the night in Gérard's hotel room, sleeping in the same bed even when Gérard was having sex with someone else.

Gérard's visit lasted seventeen days. It turned out to be the first of many that would span the better part of a decade. Like his friends who had similar friendships and romances with European men, Lambert found that his time with Gérard exposed him to the possibilities of gay life in places where homophobia was less prevalent, or at least less overt. Gérard described, for example, European capitals where gay men were free to kiss in public, and where organizations openly advocated for the human rights of sexual minorities. "That was something we hadn't talked about before," Lambert says.

For Lambert, the news that other gay communities had waged the kinds of fights he wanted to wage—and even won some of them—was revelatory, as was the notion that, however difficult things might be in Cameroon, there was an international community of sexual minorities rooting for his success. Though he had officially founded AGALES before Gérard's arrival, these conversations spurred Lambert to begin thinking more seriously about what the group might be able to achieve.

* * *

When Lambert had come up with the idea for AGALES, back in 2000, he immediately found half a dozen or so gay men who were enthusiastic about signing on. "The objective was to bring LGBT people together, in a place where they could live without being judged, without having fear, and where they could defend themselves when things happened," Stéphane says. If members of the community had trouble with the police, AGALES could advise them on how to defuse the situation. If they needed housing,

AGALES could help them find somewhere to crash. "Anything that is good for the community—that was the principal idea," Stéphane says.

Beyond the cybercafés, there were few feasible meeting spots for gay men, so many of the AGALES meetings were held at Lambert's family home. After several years living on his own, Lambert, now twenty-six, had moved back in, reclaiming the room his father had kept for him.

One of the initial goals of the group was to expand the number of places where they could gather. AGALES members began working to identify bar and restaurant owners who were sympathetic to them, or who were at least willing to look the other way to accommodate paying customers. "Today, you can be gay and go to a hetero bar, show yourself off and not have too much fear," Stéphane says, explaining how the situation has changed since that time. "If you did that before, it showed you had a strong head. But there was more fear than joy in it."

The development of a safe, accommodating social scene proved easier than expected. The lack of enforcement, or even awareness, of Article 347 bis meant there was little risk of arrest. The main threat when going out, beyond physical violence, was blackmail—if they flirted with the wrong guy, Lambert and his friends would need to pay a potentially exorbitant sum to keep him from destroying their reputations. To avoid this, they didn't explore too widely, sticking with particular bars on particular nights. By far the most important was Sunday at the Victoire.

"Ooh la la, this bar was always full," Lambert recalls. "On Sundays, the road would be blocked. There was everyone, coming from all the regions of Cameroon."

Just as important as the cultivation of a gay-friendly bar scene was the establishment of AGALES as a refuge for people who had been turned away by their families and communities. The urgency of this work only increased with the spread of HIV/AIDS among men who have sex with men, or MSM. It would be years before the government included MSM as a priority group in its national action plan to combat HIV/AIDS. In the meantime, fear of the virus combined with general homophobia meant that those who tested positive were often abandoned.

This aspect of Lambert's work goes a long way toward explaining the respect Lambert's relatives, whatever their initial reservations about his sexual orientation, now afford him. Jules, who takes pride in his identity as a man of faith, said the assistance AGALES offered to down-and-out HIV/AIDS patients, more than anything else, convinced him that Lambert was a good person and a credit to the family:

One time, a young man came here, HIV-positive, very thin, dying practically. But Lambert welcomed him, took care of him. He protected him to the point where this man regained weight, he became a friend of the family, he did a lot of things to help out around here. We call that love. That was very remarkable, you see, because religion had rejected this person. But Lambert could welcome him, show love, take care of someone sick with AIDS. That's one of the things that positively marked me and changed my way of seeing.

He contrasted Lambert's treatment of this young man with the treatment the downtrodden—and not just gay people—sometimes receive at the hands of religious leaders. "In our spiritual milieu, which I am not trying to condemn, of course, we can sing about love when you are there and when we are exploiting you, but when you are no longer useful you are rejected, ignored, banished," he says. "And that's a tough reality."

Through his work with AGALES, then, Lambert was able, almost entirely on his own, to build himself up as an activist with influence that extended beyond his gay friends. Perhaps most remarkably, Lambert's father began talking about how he wanted Lambert, even though he's the youngest child, to succeed him as head of the family when he dies.

This influence would turn out to be invaluable in the aftermath of the Victoire raid, as Lambert tried to free himself and his friends from prison and the conditions that threatened their health and safety. Though he had little sense of this while he was incarcerated, he was undertaking this effort at the beginning of an anti-gay panic the likes of which Cameroon had never before experienced.

4

Human rights
feeds on horror

As 2005 came to a close, activists did what they could to keep the case of the so-called Yaoundé 11 in the headlines.

IGLHRC, the organization that had been instrumental in bringing details of the case to the world's attention, continued to publish updates on how it was progressing and how Lambert and the other detained men were faring behind bars. On November 30, 2005, IGLHRC joined seven other organizations, including Human Rights Watch, in presenting a letter to Cameroon's justice minister urging that the men be freed (Human Rights Watch et al. 2005). "While we understand that there are important internal debates about homosexuality in Cameroonian society, these men have not been charged with any crime," the letter read, "and there is no evidence that they have broken any law."

For IGLHRC, this work had clear benefits. By associating itself with the story of the Yaoundé 11—a story marked by sympathetic protagonists, obvious villains and a grim carceral setting—the organization raised its profile, helping draw attention to, and support for, its broader mission and programming. "Our donors liked it," recalls Cary Alan Johnson, IGHLRC's Africa coordinator. "It was something that you could really wrap your head around. Kondengui prison, it was a real place. It was concrete, dramatic, if you will."

From the vantage point of Lambert and the other men stuck inside Kondengui, however, the results of the activists' interventions were more mixed. On the one hand, IGLHRC had successfully arranged for the delivery of food and other emergency assistance to the detainees, and had set them up with lawyers eager to work on their case. Yet as their time in the facility passed the six-month mark, there were no indications that the men were getting any closer to release. As the IGLHRC letter noted, they hadn't even been formally charged with anything.

In the early months of 2006, the situation became even bleaker. Thanks to an unprecedented series of high-profile scandals, the "important internal debates about homosexuality" mentioned in the letter moved to the center of Cameroon's national discourse for the first time.

* * *

To be sure, such debates were not entirely unknown in Cameroon. In the preceding decades, the country had developed a complicated relationship with its sexual minorities, one marked by tensions that can be traced back to before it attained independence in 1960.

Initially colonized by the German Empire, most of modern-day Cameroon was administered by the French following World War I. (Part of the country was under British control during this period, but it would later join with Francophone Cameroon.) The fact that the country attained its independence from Paris meant it did not inherit the same anti-gay legislation that remains on the books in former British holdings like Uganda and Kenya.

But hostility toward homosexuality ran deep among Cameroonian nationalists in the pre-independence period. In a chapter for the collection *Sexual Diversity in Africa: Politics, Theory and Citizenship*, the Cameroonian political scientist S.N. Nyeck (2013) highlights an interview in which Ngouo Woungly-Massaga, a guerrilla fighter in Cameroon's independence war, explains how homosexuality was seen as a weakness, an indulgence of an un-African practice that reflected an insufficient commitment to the nationalist cause. Sexual minorities, in this light, were compromised, having been corrupted by behavior that was associated with the outside powers that stood between the guerrillas and their liberation.

This stigma moved in multiple directions: Just as sexual minorities were assumed to be politically compromised, those who were politically compromised were often assumed to be sexual minorities, or at least to have engaged in same-sex sexual acts. Such suspicions endured well after independence and extended to the highest reaches of government. Ahmadou Ahidjo, Cameroon's first president, had been handpicked for the office by Paris and, with no liberation war credentials of his own, was accused by many Cameroonians of serving French interests more than theirs. To this day, it is also widely believed, though no proof has ever emerged, that Louis-Paul Aujoulat, a former colonial governor, sodomized Ahidjo before he took office, and in so doing allowed France to continue asserting control over an ostensibly sovereign nation.

In 1972, Ahidjo pushed through Article 347 bis, the anti-gay law that remains in effect today. The law may have represented an attempt by Ahidjo to deflect the rumors swirling around him. In addition, Basile Ndjio, a Cameroonian anthropologist who has studied the evolution of anti-gay sentiment in the country, situates the law within Ahidjo's broader effort to foster a unified national identity, a daunting task in a country that boasts more than 240 ethnic groups. "In the project of constructing a national identity, you need to have one people, one chief, one nation," Ndjio says, explaining why sexual minorities were seen as deserving of punishment. "All forms of nonconventional sexuality were seen as obstacles or handicaps to this project."

For decades, though, Article 347 bis remained little more than a gesture, an expression of a sexual conservatism that was perhaps widely shared but not strongly felt. Ndjio remembers that in his childhood neighborhood of New Bell, in Douala, gay people were mocked but generally spared more dramatic forms of abuse. Arrests, meanwhile, were almost nonexistent until the Victoire raid, which turned out to be the first of several events that transformed homosexuality into a matter of interest to the public at large.

Two other incidents occurring in quick succession proved just as important, if not more so, in focusing attention on the issue. First, on Christmas Eve 2005, the Catholic Archbishop of Yaoundé, Victor Tonyé Bakot, devoted much of his sermon to the threat posed by homosexuality, which he described as a temptation presented by "the power of money and evil forces." Bakot contended, among other things, that students were being taught to "accept and tolerate homosexuality" in schools (quoted in Human Rights Watch 2010).

Such comments from a high-profile religious leader contributed to the widespread conflation of homosexuality and pedophilia. More importantly, they reinforced the belief that sexual minorities were willing to subvert Cameroonian, and African, values in exchange for material wealth. Corruption and homosexuality, then, were becoming so closely related in the popular imagination as to be almost interchangeable.

The second incident occurred the following month. On January 30, 2006, the tabloid newspaper *Anecdote* published an article under the headline "The Top 50

Presumed Homosexuals in Cameroon," which was exactly what it sounded like: an attempt to name and shame high-profile people who had, according to the paper, engaged in same-sex sexual acts. Among those named were high-ranking government officials, athletes, journalists, businessmen, church leaders and well-known members of civil society. Other lists soon followed, both in *Anecdote* and in other publications, captivating the political class and everyone else following the story.

Nyeck (2013) writes that, because of the association of alternative sexualities with ill-gotten gains, publication of the lists was motivated as much by a desire to denounce corruption as anything else. She quotes Francois Bikoro, the editor-in-chief of *Anecdote*, as saying he wanted "a reasonable equation between the aspirations of the people and the means at the disposal of the governors." Bikoro said that those who were "corrupted" should be prosecuted, and that their wealth should be redistributed.

The tabloids presented their work as a public service performed at considerable risk. Whether or not these risks were overstated, the stories proved explosive, as stories of sex and scandal often do. According to IGLHRC, the price of individual copies of *Anecdote* "went from 300 francs to as much as 5,000 francs [US$10] on the day it printed its list, and the publishers had to make photocopies available for street sales" (Johnson 2007).

* * *

It is difficult to pin down what exactly was driving these events, or to explain why they all occurred around the same time. Was it simply a coincidence, or were they somehow related? Those who have looked into this question, Nyeck and Ndjio among them, have yet to come up with a satisfactory answer. Lambert, for his part, noted that the incidents, from the Victoire raid to Bakot's sermon and the tabloid lists, seemed to build on one another, but the initial catalysts for all of them remain obscure.

What is clear is that this period marked a turning point, after which debates about sexual minorities, and whether they should enjoy the full rights of citizenship, acquired a new kind of staying power in Cameroon.

The tabloid lists in particular, with their focus on a cross-section of the country's elites, resonated with the public to a degree that even their creators might not have anticipated. This had everything to do with the profound disconnect that has grown between the population and the government headed by President Paul Biya, who succeeded Ahidjo and has now been in power for more than thirty-five years.

For many in the country, Biya is felt, above all, as an absence. In March 2018, he made headlines for calling his first cabinet meeting since 2015, a remarkable gap for any president, let alone one confronting two separate insurgencies: from Boko Haram in the north and Anglophone separatists in the west.

He and his wife, Chantal, spend so much time in Europe that Cameroonians jokingly refer to them as "that

Swiss couple who holiday in Cameroon." In 2016, footage circulated on social media of a Cameroonian man in fatigues who planted himself outside the Intercontinental Hotel in Geneva, where Biya was believed to be staying. "What are you doing here?!" the man yelled during a ten-minute tirade that ended only after repeated efforts by hotel staff to get him to leave. "What are you doing here all the time? Why have you fled Cameroon?"

The regime's graft is legendary. Transparency International placed the country at the bottom of its Corruption Perceptions Index in 1998 and 1999. Biya reportedly owns castles in France and Germany, and media reports accused him in 2009 of spending $40,000 per night on hotel rooms for his entourage while vacationing in the south of France.

Left largely to themselves, abandoned by both the state and the multilateral institutions guiding the country's "reforms," Cameroonians build their lives in cities and towns bereft of formal opportunity. The narrow, congested streets of Douala, the biggest city, are filled with evidence of underemployment: According to one survey cited in a 2010 report by the International Crisis Group, 80 percent of the city's 50,000 motorcycle taxi drivers had high school diplomas. Half held college degrees.

In this context, the notion of a homosexual conspiracy among political and business leaders offers a tidy explanation for ordinary Cameroonians' plight as well as the state's indifference. As Nyeck (2013) writes, those who buy into the conspiracy see their country as a place where powerful men "prey on young Cameroonians and force them to participate in abominable Western pleasures." If you refuse to participate, of course your odds of advancing will be slim.

The Cameroon case, therefore, represents a reversal of the scapegoating often seen elsewhere in Africa. Whereas in places like Zimbabwe and Uganda leaders have attacked sexual minorities in order to distract the public from bad governance and inequality, in Cameroon it was the public, not the state, that first embraced homophobia to explain these same phenomena. The Cameroon case thus illustrates how anti-LGBT sentiment can vary from country to country, exposing the flaws inherent in handwringing about "African homophobia," which is often presented as uniform and immutable.

As the scandal snowballed in early 2006, Biya, eager to silence a story that challenged the credibility of his government, addressed the nation in a speech for National Youth Day. Denouncing the tabloid reports, he asserted that private affairs should remain private and stressed the need to tolerate difference. "It is not acceptable that in the name of uncontrolled rumor, we allow, as we have recently, speculation on the vices and virtues of individuals that can have unintended effects on their private lives and honor," he said (Human Rights Watch 2010).

The president's words had little effect. Three days later, according to Amnesty International (2009), someone claiming to represent a youth organization published an anonymous letter calling on all Cameroonians "to report gays and lesbians to the authorities." It was an early indication of the hostile environment the Yaoundé 11 would encounter once they got out.

* * *

In March 2006, hearings in the trial of the Yaoundé 11 finally began. Though prosecutors had had nearly ten months to work on the case, they showed up to court "badly prepared and did not present any witnesses," according to the United Nations Working Group on Arbitrary Detention, which produced a report on the case (UN 2006). Didier and another suspect were immediately released for lack of evidence. A second hearing for the remaining nine was scheduled for the following month.

At that hearing, too, the prosecution arrived empty-handed, and a judge found all the men not guilty. In a statement hailing the verdict as a "major victory for human rights," IGLHRC (2006) reported that, once it was announced, "several of the men began to cry, knowing their ordeal was about to end."

But this assessment proved overly optimistic. Ignoring the verdict, prosecutors refused to approve the suspects' release, instead ordering that they stand trial again—a development that IGLHRC's Johnson said was "nothing more than a case of double jeopardy."

During a second trial, held in June, a judge found seven of the nine men guilty, even though the prosecution essentially presented the same case. Lambert was one of the two men found not guilty; the rationale behind this was never fully explained.

In any event, the convicted men were sentenced to ten months in prison, shorter than the time they'd already served, meaning the entire group was eligible for release. On June 13, 2006, they walked out of Kondengui, twelve months and twelve days after their arrival.

Leaving the prison that night, Lambert immediately became consumed with trying to care for Alim, the Muslim clothing designer housed in Kosovo who had been preyed upon by the other inmates. While in custody, Alim had tested positive for HIV; it is unclear whether he contracted the virus before his arrest or as a result of prison rape. Though he entered Kondengui looking healthy, his condition had deteriorated gravely behind bars. For at least a month, he had been unable to stand on his own during court appearances, and his body was covered with abscesses from an unidentified skin condition.

Despite global interest in the fate of the Yaoundé 11, the men's newfound fame did not translate into funds to help them put their lives back in order. They walked out of Kondengui with next to nothing.

Lambert was about to learn an important lesson, one that, over the years, he has taken to summing up in the following phrase: "Human rights feeds on horror." What he means is that, in his experience, support from international activists is most readily available when the chances for spectacle and for scoring political points are highest. Once activists accomplish what they want—in the case of the Yaoundé 11, securing the men's release—resources disappear, and those on the ground are left to their own devices as they navigate the fallout from campaigns ostensibly conducted for their benefit.

Still in the role of group leader, yet unsure of what to do, Lambert prevailed on a friend to give them 20,000 CFA francs, or around US$40, which he distributed among the nine men who were released that night. As the group went their separate ways, he held onto 5,000 francs, or about $10, for Alim's medical treatment.

Because taxi drivers were on strike, Lambert hailed a moto-taxi for them to take to the nearest hospital. He placed Alim between himself and the driver, holding him close "so the cold wouldn't kill him."

Though he didn't have nearly enough money for the treatment Alim required, a worker at the hospital took pity on Alim, admitting him on the condition that the hospital be paid later. The next day, Lambert tried turning to Alim's relatives for help. One of his cousins came to the hospital with some food, nothing more. Lambert then traveled to the home of Alim's sister, thinking that, because she was married to a military police officer, she could come up with some money. However, when he got there, the sister told Lambert she couldn't contribute even 100 francs, though she also offered some food to take back to her brother.

The domestic activist community also had little to offer. The day after the men were released, Alice Nkom, their lawyer, was in Yaoundé for a press conference about the case. She agreed to give Lambert 80,000 francs, which covered about two-thirds of the initial bill.

Without more details about Alim's condition—details that would only be available had he received proper care—it is impossible to say whether his death was inevitable, or whether he could have been saved. Nevertheless, in Lambert's mind, the struggle to come up with funds was a decisive factor in sealing Alim's fate.

After spending three days at Alim's side, Lambert decided he couldn't stay at the hospital any longer. He hadn't showered, and he still had on the same pants and dirty, half-sleeve shirt he'd been wearing at the time of their release. He summoned Raymond, another member of the Yaoundé 11, to watch over Alim, and returned to his family home.

After cleaning himself up, Lambert helped his mother prepare for a trip out of town and accompanied her to the bus terminal. It was there that he received a call from Raymond, who told him to come immediately to the hospital. When Lambert asked why, Raymond broke down, telling him Alim had died. His body needed to be taken to the morgue.

Even in death, Alim's family, apparently ashamed by his sexual orientation and the circumstances of his incarceration, refused to come to his aid. Though Muslims should ordinarily be buried as soon as possible, Alim's relatives resisted coming to the morgue and paying to remove his body. As had been the case throughout Alim's decline, it fell to Lambert to act. "Everyone abandoned me," he says. "It was my problem."

Lambert knew Alim's uncle worked as a cook for a government minister who was also Muslim. Eventually, he managed to get a message to the minister, informing him that Alim's family was refusing to honor Alim with a proper burial. The minister intervened, and Alim's uncle went to the morgue to retrieve the body and prepare for the funeral.

To this day, Lambert has not been able to summon the will to visit his dead friend's grave. He cries every time he recounts Alim's story.

It is a story that does not seem to have traveled far beyond those it immediately affected. Johnson, the staffer at IGLHRC who worked on the case, seemed genuinely surprised when, years later, he was confronted with Lambert's criticism of the group's failure even to keep tabs on their transition to life outside Kondengui.

"We had no idea that it had been so hard to find treatment for Alim after his release," Johnson said. "I'm so sorry for that."

5

Love falls

on us

After grieving Alim, Lambert set about trying to figure
out how his incarceration would shape the rest of his life.
So much had changed in a year. Prior to the Victoire raid,
he had been open about his sexual orientation, but he
had also been fairly anonymous, meaning he could choose
how much he disclosed depending on where he was and
who he was speaking to. Now, in light of the media
coverage generated by his arrest, he had to assume that
everyone knew about him, or could easily find out. How
was he to navigate this new terrain? What did Cameroon's sudden fixation on alternative sexualities mean
for his day-to-day security? His friendships and family
life? What kind of life could he make for himself in his
home country?

In seeking out answers to these questions, Lambert embraced his new circumstances rather than trying to resurrect the old ones. One of his first moves was to rent an apartment that could serve as a base for the Yaoundé 11 as they acclimatized to life as free men. Those who had less money than he did, and who could not count on support from their families, grew to rely on this space—and, by extension, on Lambert. This allowed Lambert to continue in the den-mother role he had established for himself in Kondengui.

By 2008, Lambert had also taken on a more formal role within the country's nascent LGBT rights movement. He found work with two newly formed LGBT rights organizations based in Douala: ADEFHO, headed by Alice Nkom, the lawyer, and a new group called Alternatives-Cameroun. Lambert acted as the groups' Yaoundé representative, monitoring arrests in the city and informing the groups of sexual minorities in need of legal aid.

Around that time, Lambert sat for an interview with the French filmmaker Céline Metzger that would be included in Metzger's documentary about gay life in Cameroon entitled *Sortir du Nkuta*. *Nkuta* is a word used in Cameroon to refer to a burlap bag; among LGBT Cameroonians, the phrase *sortir du nkuta* is a rough equivalent of "coming out of the closet."

By then, Lambert was looking healthier than he had when he was incarcerated. He had regained the weight that was lost to months of barely-there, prison-issued meals, and he spoke and moved with more confidence, like a man possessed of a clear sense of himself and his mission. Addressing how he had grown since his arrest, he said: "What has profoundly changed for me is that today I feel very homo ... It was a true *sortir du nkuta*."

The events of 2005 and 2006 had had a similar effect on Yaoundé's gay scene writ large. Lambert discovered upon his release that, instead of retreating in the face of the hostile press coverage and homophobic rhetoric which defined that time, his friends on the outside, both within activist circles and beyond them, had become more emboldened. Even as the scandal surrounding the tabloid lists gained momentum in early 2006, a woman who would go on to become a close friend of Lambert's opened the first nightclub catering specifically to the city's sexual minorities, a move Lambert described as one of the most audacious he'd ever seen. Another friend opened a bar that, while welcoming of everyone, soon became exclusively gay. Although the risk of arrest was much higher—and would remain so—many Cameroonian sexual minorities seemed to have decided there was no longer any point in hiding.

This was partly due to a sense that public views on homosexuality were evolving. While anti-gay voices received the most attention during the year the Yaoundé 11 were locked up, they were not representative of the entire population. The high-profile national debate, Lambert says, actually softened many people's attitudes, reducing some of the fear built up around a group of people who had previously only been whispered about. "As people spoke more about homosexuality, values started to change slightly," Lambert says. "It was a form of acceptance, because now it was something that we talked about regularly, every day on the radio, on television. That started to create a certain tolerance."

This tolerance, such as it was, likely reinforced the decision of Lambert's family to stand by him. After two years in the rented apartment, Lambert moved back, at the urging of his parents, to the family home in Yaoundé's Essos neighborhood. When France 24 came to film a documentary on the hardships facing sexual minorities in Cameroon, Lambert's father proudly declared his support for Lambert on camera. "He's the prince, the last born!" he said, beaming as he pointed to Lambert. "Before God, we are all one." In a potent sign of Lambert's status within the family, he began constructing a separate house of his own behind the house in which he was raised (Perelman and Bodin 2014).

The decision by Lambert's family to invite him back was not motivated solely by pride in his achievements as an activist. His relatives were also concerned about his welfare. In particular, Lambert's mother, who had reconciled with his father and also moved back, wanted Lambert close by out of fear for his safety. But coming home didn't always protect Lambert from verbal and physical attacks.

Shortly after his return, Lambert constructed, as a side business, a small bar that faced the street that ran past the property. One Sunday morning, after a long night out, he was drinking with friends at the bar, toasting the birth of his neighbor's first grandchild. At some point, a boy who lived up the street approached the group and gestured to his stomach, indicating he was hungry. Lambert called the boy over, gave him 100 CFA francs and sent him away.

A little while later, the boy's mother came over in a rage, demanding to know why Lambert had given her son money. She accused Lambert of trying to seduce the child, shouting so loudly she couldn't hear his denials. "We were all surprised, my friends and me," Lambert says. "I stayed calm. She finished speaking and turned her back." Instead of walking away, however, the woman turned around again, picked up an empty beer bottle and smashed it over Lambert's head, sending blood running down his face. Lambert still tried to remain calm, but when the woman moved to stab him with a piece of glass he stood up and forced her to the ground, only getting off when the woman's brother intervened.

According to Simon, a longtime friend, such incidents, combined with the emotional scars from his time in Kondengui, have given Lambert a hardness he didn't have when he was younger. Simon, who is bisexual but keeps that information closely guarded, thinks Lambert would be happier if he, too, lived more discreetly. But he understands that Lambert's conception of himself and his responsibilities as an activist would not allow for that. "He is very passionate, and Africa is not ready for that," Simon says. "Not just Cameroon, *Africa* is not ready for people like Lambert."

Lambert hopes that Simon is wrong. And on many days—when the discrimination they encounter is, if not eliminated, relegated deep into the background—he and his fellow activists can convince themselves that's the case. This is especially true when their work is going well, and they have a sense they are advancing the goals around which many of them now structure their time.

* * *

In the first decade after his release, the nature of this work underwent a profound evolution, one that reflected the collision of international priorities and domestic needs.

The case of the Yaoundé 11, which in many ways launched Cameroon's LGBT rights movement, gave international organizations an obvious cause to rally around: the repeal of Article 347 bis, Cameroon's anti-gay law. This cause has remained a central demand of foreign activists who continue to follow the situation in Cameroon, often topping their lists of recommendations for Biya's government.

Unsurprisingly, local activists also took up the mission of legal reform. For some, like Nkom, it was seen as the ultimate achievement, the end goal to which all their work was building.

Many others, though, expanded their objectives, having recognized that the law wasn't everything, and that there were other, less headline-ready changes they could be pushing for at the same time. These quieter efforts would involve defending rights—freedom of association, for example, and access to justice and health care—that are ostensibly available to everyone but are sometimes denied based on sexual orientation or gender identity.

This evolution began early. The case of Alim Mongoche made clear that people imprisoned under Article 347 bis were likely to be in desperate need of support once they got out, especially if they faced ostracization by family and friends. "We noticed that each time people were liberated from New Bell prison in Douala, when they left, they were zombies," says Parfait Behen, president of Alternatives-Cameroun. "They were sick, they'd been raped, they'd been beaten. They'd been dehumanized." To improve the chances that these people would be able to recover from the trauma of their incarceration, groups like Alternatives-Cameroun took the lead in trying to provide them with money and a place to stay.

These groups also began partnering with donor governments and international organizations involved in treating and preventing HIV/AIDS. As was the case throughout the region, this would become an area of specialization for gay male activists in Cameroon for two reasons. First, the epidemic posed a singular, potentially existential threat to their community, one the government didn't have the capacity to counter on its own, even if it had been inclined to. Second, because the government was so overwhelmed, it was willing to accept help even from organizations that advocated equal rights for sexual minorities, a position that was widely seen as violating Cameroonian law.

This created space for Cameroonian activists, Lambert among them, to engage in public programming, offering a relatively safe way to increase their visibility. One of Lambert's proudest achievements is working alongside donors to persuade Biya's government to include men who have sex with men as a target population under the national HIV/AIDS action plan. The milestone represented a clear break from the official erasure with which the country's LGBT population had long been threatened.

The obstacles to legal reform, meanwhile, remain formidable. This was evident most recently in June 2016, when Cameroonian lawmakers took up the matter of updating the penal code for the first time in decades. While the revisions touched on a number of contentious issues, including sexual harassment, adultery and political protest, Article 347 bis was not among them.

In private, some lawmakers questioned whether policing alternative sexualities should be an official priority. In public, however, not one was willing to take this position. As a result, the only objection to preserving Article 347 bis came from officials who wanted to see the maximum prison term doubled from five years to ten. When the new penal code was passed, the article was unchanged.

As the penal code was being discussed, it triggered another brief spike in public expressions of anti-gay sentiment. Alternatives-Cameroun reported that in the run-up to the vote, photos of several of the group's staffers were widely shared on social media, accompanied by slurs and threats (Erasing 76 Crimes 2016).

On its face, then, the revision process appeared to amount to a significant setback for Lambert and his peers, or at least a worrying sign of stagnation for their movement. But while it is true that the ultimate breakthrough—securing the legal right for Cameroonian sexual minorities to live uncompromisingly as themselves—remains elusive, it is wrong to suggest there has been no, or even limited, progress. Even during periods when arrests have been rampant, Lambert says, he and his peers have continued putting dents in taboos that, for many years, precluded any sort of open discussion about sexual minorities' place in society. The tactics they use are proof of the advances they've made. "There were years when we were afraid to even hold a meeting," he says. "Now, we can hold a march."

* * *

Even for the most positive activists, however, certain setbacks are so disheartening as to make faith in a better future seem naive, even delusional. This was the case for two deaths that occurred in quick succession several years ago, long after Lambert assumed his movement's worst days were behind it.

The first was the murder in 2013 of Eric Ohena Lembembe, a journalist and activist who was working, at the time of his death, as executive director of the Camer-oonian Foundation for AIDS (CAMFAIDS), a Yaoundé-based LGBT human rights organization. Lambert had known Eric, who was six years his junior, for many years, and had housed Eric for long stretches as he was trying to establish himself.

Eric had risen to become a prominent voice in the Cameroonian movement. Friends affectionately referred to him as "Princess Erica" because of his fashionable clothes and ease with friends and strangers, but he exhib-ited a dogged tenacity in his reporting and in his interac-tions with Cameroonian officials. Neela Ghoshal (2013), a senior researcher on LGBT rights for Human Rights Watch, recalled his "David versus Goliath spirit" during a meeting they had with seven members of Cameroon's military police. While the uniformed men could dismiss Ghoshal's descriptions of anti-gay abuses as the rantings of an ill-informed American, they had a harder time brushing off Eric, who called them out on their callousness. "Let's be serious," Eric said, according to Ghoshal. "We all know that gay people exist in Cameroon. In fact, they exist in all of our families. And we all know that they are mistreated. Would you tolerate this abuse if this were your brother? Would you laugh at it, if this were your sister?"

Eric was not naive to the danger these confrontations might put him in. In early July 2013, he was quoted in a statement condemning the lack of an official response to attacks on the offices of LGBT human rights groups:

There is no doubt: anti-gay thugs are targeting those who support equal rights on the basis of sexual orientation and gender identity. Unfortunately, a climate of hatred and bigotry in Cameroon, which extends to high levels in government, reassures homophobes that they can get away with these crimes. (Human Rights Watch 2013)

Two weeks later, Eric missed a Saturday work meeting, a highly unusual occurrence that sparked concern among his friends. When they still couldn't get in touch with him by Monday, they went to his apartment. The door was locked, but through a window they could see Eric's lifeless body, which showed signs of torture. His neck and feet appeared to be broken, and parts of his body appeared to have been burned white with an iron.

Lambert felt like he had lost a son. The response from the government only compounded his despair. Though Eric was the most prominent LGBT rights activist to have been murdered on the continent in at least two years, and though his death made headlines internationally, the authorities conducted a rudimentary investigation. The only people detained in connection with the case were friends and colleagues of Eric, whom police briefly held on suspicion that they were somehow involved. Publicly, officials downplayed the significance of the killing, suggesting it was a product not of homophobia but of circumstances specific to Eric's life—circumstances they never bothered to explain. "Look at the details of this person's life and you will understand why he died," Cameroon's ambassador to Geneva told the UN Human Rights Council, without elaborating (UN 2013).

But even as Cameroonian activists raged at the government, they reserved some of their most pointed comments for their international partners—the organizations that funded their work and exerted significant influence over the forms it could take. In a statement issued one week after Eric's body was found, four Cameroonian organizations, including CAMFAIDS and Alternatives-Cameroun, announced they were temporarily suspending their activities, having determined that the security situation was too dangerous. The statement, addressed to partners including the United States Agency for International Development and the Global Fund to Fight AIDS, Tuberculosis and Malaria, said they had been deprived of "a minimum level of security, institutional support and financial support" (Erasing 76 Crimes 2013).

The message was obvious: activists were increasingly reluctant to put their lives on the line in the service of programming driven by outsiders, regardless of where the money for that programming came from. "We reject a partnership that reduces our associations to simply a labor force that must work in precarious, dangerous conditions," the statement said.

* * *

The second death hit Lambert even harder. The victim in this case was a man the global LGBT rights community had promoted as a prime example of who it was trying to help, only to abandon him just as quickly.

In 2011, this man, Roger Mbede, went to the Cameroonian presidency in Yaoundé to apply for a job. After he left, he sent a series of text messages to an official he'd met there. The first message addressed the official as "Tonton," a term of respect meaning "Uncle," before making Roger's intentions clear. "I feel an attraction for men," it read. "I feel a desire to sleep with men and I am attracted by your beauty."

The message he received in return is not included in police reports from the case. But whatever the official's response, it does not appear to have been positive. Roger decided to forge ahead anyway. "Each time that I've spoken with you, I've fallen under your charm. I have fallen in love with you," he wrote. "It's wounding but I need to tell you so as not to suffer too much … Please don't be angry."

The man responded by requesting a meeting, then tipping off the military police. Two plainclothes officers arrested Roger not long after he showed up. On the strength of the messages, they prepared a report accusing him of "attempted homosexuality."

Roger appeared before judicial officials one week after his arrest. He had no lawyer, making it easier for prosecutors to secure a conviction, and a three-year sentence, under Article 347 bis. Roger would serve his time in

Kondengui, the same facility where Lambert and the rest of the Yaoundé 11 had been held six years earlier.

Foreign activists soon got wind of Roger's case, and they immediately identified it as a chance to bring global attention to the plight of sexual minorities in Cameroon. As lawyers prepared an appeal, Amnesty International named Roger a prisoner of conscience, and the organization's Write for Rights campaign generated up to 500 letters of support a day from all over the world, according to Nkom, who worked on Roger's behalf. Various organizations emphasized the flimsiness of the charges against Roger. The materials they distributed pertaining to the case often featured his photograph and the words "I'm very much in love with you"—a mistranslation of the texts that had got him in trouble.

International campaigners maintain that, after his arrest, Roger was eager to go public with his case despite the fact that the attention would surely compound the stigma he faced. "He was very clear about the importance for him for the world to know that, in Cameroon, what got him in jail was this one text," says Guillaume Bonnet, who at the time was working for the New York-based organization All Out, which launched several campaigns that drew on Roger's story. "He was doing that for him, but also for all of his brothers and sisters in Cameroon … He didn't want them to go through the same pain."

But Roger had no experience as an activist, and in retrospect it is doubtful he was prepared to embrace a struggle larger than his own. In a letter to Nkom written from Kondengui, Roger indicated that he wanted only to keep his head down until his prison term was over. "It is with eyes filled with tears and a heart completely saddened that I write you this letter," he began, lamenting that the system seemed stacked against him. "Please go cancel the appeal. I don't want to suffer any more from constant persecution from my enemies."

By this point, though, it was too late; the events that would transform Roger into a mini-celebrity were already in motion.

Like the Yaoundé 11 before him, Roger fared badly in custody. Verbal harassment from guards and inmates increased as time went on, and he endured regular physical attacks. During one of these incidents, he was smacked in the head with a wooden bench, a blow that left a scar on his brow.

His health also deteriorated. In his letter to Nkom, Roger reported losing weight "to the point where I no longer feel like myself," and said that he was "in danger." A prison-issued document chronicling Roger's various health problems offers what is surely an incomplete account of his decline. The notes appear in a doctor's scrawl on the lined pages of a red notebook: "dizziness" and a headache on January 23, 2012; "a traumatic wound" sustained in a fight at some point in 2012 (the precise date is illegible); "intense" testicular pain caused by a hernia in March 2012, followed by similar entries in April, May and June.

By July, Roger's condition was so bad, and the international outcry over his treatment so intense, that authorities decided to grant him provisional release so that he could receive the care he needed. He underwent surgery for the testicular hernia, but the procedure was not entirely successful, according to friends and activists. He also tested positive for HIV. It was unclear where he contracted it, and he never got on a treatment plan.

Roger nevertheless remained optimistic about the new beginning offered by his release, even though his appeal was still pending. By far the most bookish member of his family, he was eager to complete his master's degree at Yaoundé's Catholic University of Central Africa, where he was studying the philosophy of education. "He was very keen to finish his studies. That's one thing he really wanted to do," says Jean-Eric Nkurikiye, a Burundian campaigner with Amnesty International who worked on Roger's case.

Roger soon discovered, though, that any attempt to return to his normal life would be complicated by his newfound notoriety. The university, for one thing, had become a hostile environment. A friend recalls that someone posted a sign on Roger's door that read "Dirty *Pédé*," and Amnesty reported that he was later assaulted by four unknown men just off campus (Corey-Boulet 2015).

Fearing for his safety, Roger moved in with Lambert, staying at the house in Essos. After three months there, he moved again, this time to the home of the aunt and uncle who had raised him, on the outskirts of Yaoundé.

The decision suggested that he was still figuring out what kind of life he wanted. Though he was primarily attracted to men, he sometimes slept with women, and had fathered a son about ten years before. When he returned to his childhood home, he was accompanied by a woman who identified as a lesbian but, in need of a place to stay, had agreed to pose as Roger's girlfriend. Roger told his family he was no longer gay. The woman, who asked not to be named, would become pregnant with Roger's second child within six months.

* * *

None of this ambiguity appeared in any of the material that groups like All Out continued to produce about Roger's case. Now that he was out of prison, these groups took advantage of the opportunity to get Roger on camera, telling his story to the world—or at least a version of it.

"We thought his story was so powerful in the sense that it really encapsulated, I think, sort of the unfairness and also the lack of logic around the anti-gay law," says Andre Banks, who was then working as All Out's executive director. Human Rights Watch, which featured Roger's case in a 2013 report detailing abuses related to Article 347 bis, viewed the case similarly. "The fact that it was an innocuous message that was used as evidence against him and also a message expressing affection—it kind of encapsulated in that particular story everything that was wrong with Cameroon and their targeting of the LGBT community," says Graeme Reid, director of the organization's LGBT rights program.

But while international organizations were quick to associate themselves with Roger, they were slow to take the steps that might have saved his life. In December 2012, the International Lesbian, Gay, Bisexual, Trans and Intersex Association, a global federation pushing for sexual minority rights, held its world conference in Stockholm. By that point, most activists were aware of Roger's case and concerned for his welfare. Conference organizers decided to invite Roger as a "special guest," knowing he would then seek asylum, according to Thomas Fouquet Lapar, a French activist. The idea was hatched late, however, and it was not possible to process Roger's visa application in time, Lapar says.

On December 17, the day after the conference came to a close, an appeals court upheld Roger's guilty verdict. Roger went into hiding, and his ambiguous legal status complicated subsequent efforts to get him out of Cameroon.

Nkurikiye, the Amnesty campaigner, says Roger's conviction made it illegal for him to leave, meaning the organization was in no position to help, as it could not carry out an intervention in violation of local laws. But Michel Togué, a lawyer who also worked on Roger's case, says Cameroonian authorities would have needed to issue a specific order barring Roger from traveling if they didn't want him going anywhere. There is no evidence they did so.

In late 2012, a regional organization, the Central Africa Human Rights Defenders Network, drew up budgets for two possible escape plans for Roger, both of which involved overland travel to Chad to avoid altercations with airport authorities, who were more likely than border officers to stop Roger. From Chad, he would fly either to Europe or the United States. However, Patience Freida, who works on LGBT issues for the organization, says it lost contact with Roger while the budgets were being approved. "There was a bit of negligence in this case," she says. Because members had no news of Roger, she adds, "We said to ourselves, 'He must be out of danger.'"

In fact, Roger believed his situation was becoming more precarious. In a January 2013 email to an activist at All Out, he reported having received a letter the previous week—it was apparently "slipped under his door"—that included a threat: "Be very careful and don't be stupid. You risk losing your life, while those who are encouraging you will remain living."

Getting desperate, Lapar turned to Dignity for All, a program run by a consortium of human rights organizations that provides emergency assistance to activists and human rights defenders endangered because of their work on LGBT issues. The program was created in September 2012 and receives significant funding from the US State Department. Lapar says Dignity approved Roger's case and agreed to provide him with about $5,000, more than enough to pay for his travel, but the money was not disbursed until August 2013.

The plan then was for Roger to travel to France. But Dignity for All does not provide help with the visa process, and the French Embassy in Yaoundé dragged its feet. Lapar, who is based in France, says he found little help on the ground in Cameroon as he tried to get Roger's papers in order. Local organizations had few resources and little influence, and international groups failed to coordinate their efforts, wasting valuable time.

To Lapar, this inability to mobilize at a time when Roger was most in need of assistance reflects poorly on the priorities of global activists:

> I was bothered by the inaction or the useless action of many players, and for me this case of Roger is quite illustrative of how the global human rights movement—not just LGBTI—can be sadly, I don't know, inert. People can say a lot of things—"Oh, we're so indignant about the sentence that he faced"—but when it's just about picking up a phone and calling an ambassador of a country to say we need this guy to be out, no one does it. And it's so easy.

Lambert was angry too, though hardly surprised. Foreign activists had succeeded in getting Roger out of prison, a concrete deliverable they could parade before their own donors. Why wouldn't they move on to the next emergency? The similarities to the story of Alim Mongoche were painfully obvious; to Lambert, it was "human rights feeds on horror" all over again.

It is fair to ask whether it should fall to international activists to manage a case like Roger's. Ideally, local organizations would have been able to arrange and carry out a plan to guarantee Roger's safety. Yet in reality, Cameroonian organizations working on LGBT issues receive their funding from foreign donors, and this informs the work they can do: money is earmarked specifically for HIV/AIDS programming, for example, or legal aid. The members of these organizations are often quite poor themselves. As one Yaoundé-based activist told me, local groups did whatever they could to help Roger with his individual requests for handouts. But it does not appear any of them had funds that could have been used to make a significant difference in his security or living situation.

Moreover, Roger had decided he had no future in Cameroon. The only hope, he believed, was for him to start a new life elsewhere. And the international donors, diplomats and activists who were best positioned to make this new life possible—the same people who had spent more than a year voicing their concern about Roger's situation—failed to mobilize when it mattered.

* * *

On December 12, 2013, David Cicilline, the Democratic congressman from Rhode Island, took to the floor of the US House of Representatives to deliver a one-minute statement about Roger in honor of Human Rights Day. "I pledge to continue to follow his story and do what I can to secure his safety," he said.[1]

At around that time, on the other side of the Atlantic, the French Embassy in Yaoundé finally granted Roger his visa, allowing him to fulfill his dream of leaving Cameroon. Roger would never use it. He had just one month to live.

There are competing versions of how Roger's final weeks unfolded. In the most widely accepted account, Roger's family removed him from the hospital and held him in the village against his will, waiting for him to die. The source of this information is Lambert, who went to the village in early January, days before Roger's death, for a visit that quickly turned chaotic.

Soon after Lambert arrived, dozens of people gathered around as members of Roger's family questioned Lambert about their relationship as well as the extensive interest in their relative's case. Lambert felt threatened. Two of Roger's cousins had machetes, he says, adding that they kept him there "for nearly ten hours."

At no point was Lambert permitted to see Roger. Lambert says he left the village convinced the family had decided to let Roger die. Several days after Roger's death, which was confirmed on January 10, 2014, Lambert told the Associated Press (2014) that, during the course of his visit, family members "said they were going to remove the homosexuality which is in him"—a claim that is central for those who say Roger's death was the direct result of his family's homophobia.

Today, though, Lambert says that because of the general confusion of the scene, he doesn't remember anyone saying those things in so many words. "Nobody said that explicitly," he says. While his broad claims may be accurate, then, his version of events is far from the definitive account that foreign activists would later portray it as being.

Noel, a cousin with whom Roger was particularly close, provides a different version of what happened. He says he understands why Lambert may have been intimidated during the confrontation. But he claims that Roger's relatives were simply trying to understand what was at the root of his health problems to see if there was any way to help. Noel denies his family wanted Roger dead. Instead, he says, Roger's death can be attributed solely to their inability to get him adequate medical care.

The woman who was posing as Roger's girlfriend might have been able to provide a thorough, neutral account of Roger's final days. But she had left the village several weeks before, just four days after giving birth to their daughter. She says she was trying to find a place where Roger could recover from his illness, since he seemed to be faring poorly at home.

What she does recall, however, undercuts Noel's claim that Roger faced no threat in the village. She says she remembers getting a call from Noel a few days before Roger's death, warning her to stay away. She says Noel told her there were certain members of his family who thought Roger was cursed and might harm him. This woman says she is not surprised Noel neglected to disclose this information himself, citing his apparent wish to protect his family's reputation.

It is perhaps too much to expect such divergent recollections to yield satisfactory answers. Given how much time has passed, and the absence of an official investigation, it may prove impossible to ever determine which story—Lambert's or Noel's—is closer to the truth.

Roger was buried hastily in his family's village, in a makeshift coffin cobbled together with wooden planks. Noel suggested waiting to see if international organizations would send money for a proper service, but the family concluded this was unlikely, given what was being said about them, and they were reluctant to continue paying to keep his body in the morgue. They decided to just get on with it.

Activists honored him in different ways. All Out organized a "virtual vigil": a petition calling on world leaders to do away with anti-gay laws. In Cameroon, one LGBT organization hung paintings of Roger in its office. Another named a conference room after him.

These gestures mean little to his friends. The lack of help on the part of Roger's foreign contacts in honoring someone who attracted so much attention while he was alive is an enduring mystery for the family, Noel says. "The entire world knew my brother. Ambassadors, everyone," he says. "If they didn't do anything for his death, well, that really disappointed me."

Noel says Roger's aunt, especially, wonders how someone who became so well-known had, apparently, been forgotten so quickly. "She asks until today, 'With all the relations he had, with all of his friends, what kind of friends are they?'"

* * *

The deaths of Eric and Roger were dramatic losses, but they are far from the only ones Lambert has suffered in the years since he walked free from Kondengui. The ranks of his generation of sexual minorities have been thinned, in many cases, by the same problems that afflict many Cameroonians, chiefly poverty and inadequate health care. Yet the individual stories of Lambert's fellow detainees underscore the fact that certain challenges are, if not specific to the gay community, more impactful on its members' well-being and survival. In addition to Alim Mongoche, three other men have died of what were believed to be AIDS-related complications. Another long ago fled to Europe, having convinced himself there was no way he could live safely in his home country. The Yaoundé 11 have been whittled down to six.

The generation of sexual minorities to come of age since 2005 is, despite the persistent threat of legal repercussions, more visible than their predecessors in many ways. They have Lambert to thank for this, a fact that many of them seem to appreciate. As much as anyone else, he initiated the conversations that made visibility possible, and showed them how to shoulder it. When asked to describe him, the most common word these young men, women and transgender activists reach for, by far, is "icon." The meetings they convene are nothing if not lively, marked by bawdy jokes, petty squabbles and near-constant side chatter. But when Lambert raises his voice to speak, he commands their focus and respect.

Yet there are important differences between Lambert and this new crop of activists, both in style and emphasis. These differences reflect how the landscape they're operating in has changed. Whereas Lambert and other sexual minorities his age had to scream to get the world's attention, his younger peers know that they have it now; few people in Cameroon would make the argument today that Cameroonian sexual minorities don't exist. Having formed a semi-cohesive movement and identified allies in civil society, the government and the diplomatic corps, they are now focused on trying to use that attention most effectively—a focus that sometimes comes off as trying to behave as politely and inoffensively as possible for fear that what little influence they've been able to marshal could vanish at any time.

Brice Evina, the current president of CAMFAIDS, describes the difference this way: whereas Lambert acted primarily out of passion, younger activists are more strategic.

"The present generation thinks they can do better. They think they can critique what has been done in the past," he says. "Lambert's work was more emotional. He feels these things. And he launches himself in the fight without thinking, 'Is this going to work? Will there be consequences?'"

Evina goes on:

> The fight led by Lambert and the others who came up with him has been necessary. It's them who have permitted us to open people's eyes. But we have a different approach. We are trying to help the government understand the situation we are in, to understand that we are not extraterrestrials, to understand that we are all one, all the same, and that it's nothing but a sexuality. That's the difference between us and the past generation. The past generation was more confrontational.

These tensions aside, the Cameroonian LGBT rights movement remains the most important thing in Lambert's life. His closest friends are fellow activists or other members of the LGBT community who benefit from the work that activists do. These relationships, he says, take the place of a long-term romantic partnership, which has never been much of a priority. That is not to say Lambert would spurn love if it came his way; he just doesn't actively seek it out. "We don't fall in love," he says, explaining his approach. "Love falls on us."

Simon and other friends of Lambert worry that, because of his high-profile identification with an issue that remains controversial, he will never be able to find true peace in Cameroon. They think he should instead consider taking advantage of his contacts within the global activist movement to relocate to Europe or the United States. Lambert acknowledges that such a move wouldn't be too hard for him to arrange.

But unlike many of his peers, he has never dreamed of seeking refuge elsewhere. During the time since the raid at the Victoire, he has invested too much, both personally and professionally, to abandon the fight for sexual minority rights now. "There is a lot of work to do here," he says. "I helped nearly all of the associations that are in Cameroon to strengthen themselves. I want to be there when we are able to shout the first cry of joy that we are free. I want to be there, to build something until the end."

PART 2
CÔTE D'IVOIRE

6

Here in the
realm of art

The story of the Yaoundé 11 was one of the biggest stories of any kind to come out of Cameroon in 2005. It came to define, for outsiders as well as some insiders, what life was like for sexual minorities in the country. The media coverage had been so loud, and the ramifications of the story so layered, that it was widely treated like the only recent event that had been of any consequence. In this way, it seemed to represent an entire world.

Yet the story by no means captured the full picture of that world—not in 2005, or at any other time. That same year, on the other side of Yaoundé, to take just one example that cut against the headlines, a man in his early thirties had dived headlong into the most fulfilling same-sex relationship of his life. His immersion in that relationship was so total that everything else going on in the city—the arrests, the trials, the unhinged reporting in the local tabloids—registered only on the outer margins of his mind, and often not even there.

It had taken that that man—whose name is Brahima, and whose home country is Côte d'Ivoire—many long years to reach the point where such a relationship might be possible. Though he had become romantically involved with two men while he was still living in his native Abidjan, he'd decided at a certain point that the risks associated with pursuing a life as a man who loves men in Ivorian society were simply too high. Instead, he'd met and fallen in love with a Cameroonian girl named Muriel, who was in Côte d'Ivoire pursuing her studies. After Muriel gave birth to their daughter in 2002, Brahima decided to follow her back to Douala, Cameroon's damp, dilapidated, impossibly lively port city and economic center.

Brahima did not last long there. Everything about life in Douala turned out to be a disappointment. A few months before he arrived, his own country had been sliced in two following a failed coup attempt, with rebels taking control of its northern half and crippling its economy. Cameroon, by contrast, was at peace; yet Brahima found the city's infrastructure in shambles and job opportunities lacking. After years of making handsome profits selling motorcycle parts throughout Côte d'Ivoire, he tried and failed to establish himself in Douala's jewelry trade before resorting to living off his savings. His relationship with Muriel soured after he started sleeping with an older woman, and the drama around their split eventually convinced him that he had no choice but to leave.

He made it to Yaoundé just a few months before the raid at the Victoire that ensnared Lambert and the others. By Brahima's own account, he was directionless, and Thierry, the Cameroonian man who would become his lover and partner, was among the first people he met. The personal turbulence back in Douala from which Brahima was fleeing made the ease of Yaoundé, with its gentle hills and relative calm, all the more welcoming. Things moved quickly, as though someone had planned them in advance. Not long after they were first introduced, Thierry offered to let Brahima move into his family's expansive home so he could stop spending money on hotel rooms. They started passing all their free time together, and sleeping together, soon after that.

Thierry's family seemed not to concern themselves with his private life, so the new couple could move as they wished between the house and the various bars they frequented throughout the city. Brahima has a faint recollection of hearing reports that people were being arrested on suspicion of committing same-sex sexual acts, but he never felt in danger himself. He simply followed Thierry's lead when choosing who to talk to and who to avoid, trusting his partner to keep him safe. In the months they were together, he allowed himself to live more openly with another man than he'd ever dreamed of in Abidjan, where his family lived, or Douala, where Muriel might have observed him. "When you are far from your family, you are free to do what you want, as you want," he says. "I could pursue it 100 percent because I didn't have pressure."

The disconnect between Brahima's life and what was generally understood to be the story of gay life in Cameroon at the time highlights the mistake inherent in conceiving of sexual minorities in one city, or one country, or anywhere, as a kind of monolith—living, loving and struggling together. Rather, it was precisely Brahima's ability to distance himself from the more visible elements of Yaoundé's gay scene that enabled him to give himself over to his relationship with Thierry, even amid a moral panic over men who do what the two of them were doing in Thierry's room.

His position in relation to the community was hardly unusual. Brahima was merely living as most sexual minorities in the region did before gay liberation movements came into fashion, and as many still do today: underground, and out of sight.

* * *

Brahima was born in 1971 into a family of seven children in the neighborhood of Williamsville, in Abidjan's Adjamé district. Located north of the Ebrié Lagoon and the bright, commanding skyline of the city center, the neighborhood offered less of what attracted foreigners to Abidjan and more of what attracted Ivorians: affordable housing, high-functioning infrastructure and access to the beating heart of an economy that had long set their country apart as a kind of regional jewel.

The son of a woodworker and a housewife, Brahima showed, from an early age, the drive and ambition that could enable someone to do great things in Abidjan, though he would later come to regret the ways he applied it.

As a young student, Brahima managed to secure a spot in one of the city's premier high schools, the Collège Moderne de Cocody, where he studied alongside the sons and daughters of government ministers and other dignitaries. Brahima had less money than his peers, but he was determined to keep up with them socially. He stayed on top of the latest fashions, going through endless pairs of Sebago shoes, and made sure he had enough money to go out after class, even if it required stealing from his parents. "My problem is, I don't hesitate to approach people who impress me," he says. "I wanted to learn about them. And that's how I got to know a lot of people."

Among the people he got to know was Stéphane Hamidou Doukouré, a young man of considerable privilege who was said to have family ties, however distant, to the country's founding president, Félix Houphouët-Boigny. Years later, among the Ivorian diaspora in Paris, Doukouré would reinvent himself as Douk Saga, pioneer of the drum machine-driven *coupé-décalé*, or scam-and-scram, musical genre that remains Abidjan's main cultural export. Even as a high school student, Doukoré embodied the hard-living hustle that would one day make him *coupé-décalé*'s chief ambassador. Brahima followed his lead: skipping class to hang out in outdoor maquis restaurants, or spending weekends sipping whiskey and champagne in Abidjan's most garish nightclubs.

Grades were a secondary concern for this crowd, and Brahima soon stopped worrying about them, too. But what he didn't fully appreciate was that many of his peers had an elite safety net that he would never be able to rely on. When he and his friends failed exams necessary to stay on track for their diplomas, his friends worked family connections to get into other schools or start their careers. Brahima, meanwhile, was forced to retreat to Williamsville.

Brahima would eventually blame this period, and the fact that he missed out on a diploma, for his chronic financial insecurity, which has hounded him into his forties. "We played with our lives," he says. "We had the luck to live in a certain neighborhood, but we could have gone even further than that. We attacked this life of joy a bit too early."

Though he has never been destitute, Brahima has also never stayed on solid financial ground for very long. His poverty has generated all the usual hardships, along with one more: it has, he says, deprived him of the social status necessary to explore his sexuality freely. But that is another thing he didn't fully appreciate until it was too late to do much about it.

* * *

For several weeks in early 1997, Brahima observed his first boyfriend from a distance. They frequented the same clothing store in Adjamé, spending each visit going through stacks of newly arrived muscle shirts and Chicago Bulls jerseys. They exchanged polite smiles, nothing more, until one day when the man entered wearing a brown Harley-Davidson T-shirt featuring a cartoon drawing of a biker in a cowboy hat. Brahima was enamored of "the American style, the Texas style." He said to the store's owner, "I'm looking for a T-shirt like that, but in another color." The owner didn't have one in stock, so he called the man over, and Brahima took the opportunity to compliment him. "Your style is nice," Brahima said. "I see you as well," the man responded, "and your style is nice."

The man's name was Woulai Bah, and he worked as a cook at the Sofitel, which in those days was located in Abidjan's downtown Plateau district, near the highway that bordered the lagoon. This was before cell phones came into wide use, so Woulai Bah would search for Brahima in Adjamé each night after work. Together they would head back to Woulai Bah's apartment to eat chicken and cake pilfered from the Sofitel's kitchen. They developed a close emotional, though not physical, friendship. Woulai Bah disclosed that he was gay, sensing Brahima would not judge even though Brahima had revealed little about his own private life. "He knew that I was one of the rare people who would understand," Brahima says.

Brahima had never had a friend who acknowledged sleeping with men, let alone one who identified as gay. He was surprised to observe that Woulai Bah lived a fairly ordinary life, and had even attained some success. He seemed to have all the things Brahima was chasing—things that, in the context of a deteriorating economy, were likely to remain out of reach for an unskilled high school dropout like himself: a steady job, an apartment, nice clothes, independence. "Bizarrely, his life was better arranged than people who were not homosexual," Brahima says. Woulai Bah's only apparent problem was loneliness. "I had a sense of someone who needed friends, who needed people," Brahima says. "Someone maybe like me."

After about a year, Brahima began to develop romantic feelings for Woulai Bah, the first he'd ever felt for a man. "I will say that he really initiated me," Brahima says.

We understood each other well—that was the first thing. The second thing was that he had habits that were very attractive. He had the courage to tell me about his situation. He was very attentive. I felt very good when I was with him. Before him, men did not attract me. I never thought that a man could react like a woman—could be comforting, attentive, kind, helpful.

One night, Brahima was going through Woulai Bah's magazines and discovered a stash of gay pornography.

"So it's two men in the photos making love like that?" he remembers asking. He had never seen anything like it. It was all the inspiration he needed. Before long, Brahima and Woulai Bah embarked on their own sexual relationship.

This unexpected turn led Brahima down a road of confused second-guessing that has never really ended. "'Brahima, you are with Woulai Bah. Is it really like that?'" he recalls asking himself at the time. "I asked myself a lot of questions related to what I had just discovered, my sexuality. 'What are people going to think of me if they learn about this? What will my family think about this?'" On the one hand, he agreed with Woulai Bah's argument that sexuality was a matter of personal liberty. "What he said was just and true," Brahima says. "He used to say, 'That's what I do. Why do others complain?'" On the other hand, Brahima had continued dating, and sleeping with, women all this time. One of his girlfriends had recently given birth to his first child, a baby girl, and he feared becoming a source of shame for her.

After about four months, the doubting overwhelmed everything Brahima liked about the relationship. "It was stronger than me," he says. He started going over to Woulai Bah's less and less. When Woulai Bah asked what was wrong, Brahima couldn't bring himself to explain. "I preferred that he understand on his own," he says. He responded that he had simply been "busy," but the relationship never recovered, and the two men lost contact.

Woulai Bah eventually quit his post at the Sofitel and moved to Europe, something Brahima only learned when he went looking for him months later. They haven't spoken or seen each other since, and Brahima now regrets how he let the relationship end. "Today, I say to myself that we had a lot of things between us that went really well," he says. "So yes, I regret it sometimes."

* * *

Brahima would have one more relationship with a man before Muriel came into his life. He met this second man, Rodrigue, at one of the gay-friendly bars Woulai Bah had shown him: Le Dollar, in Plateau's Dokui neighborhood. In some ways, Rodrigue was immediately familiar. Like Woulai Bah, he worked as a chef and shared Brahima's enthusiasm for Abidjan street fashion. But he was also discreet—so discreet, in fact, that when Brahima first disclosed, over drinks, that he slept with men, Rodrigue merely smiled. He only acknowledged he was gay a few days later, when the pair were chatting with a mutual friend. "And that's how things started," Brahima says.

Compared to the relationship with Woulai Bah, this one burned less brightly, as Brahima and Rodrigue only saw each other a few times a week. Their time together was also different in another respect: instead of passing nights alone in an apartment, they often met each other out in the city, at the bars and private parties that formed the city's nascent gay scene. Brahima still struggled with the

doubting and questioning that had doomed his relationship with Woulai Bah, but now this struggle was eased by
the fact that, for the first time in his life, he felt connected
to a wider community.

A number of factors had aligned to give this community space to grow. First, as a former French colony, Côte
d'Ivoire had not inherited a law criminalizing same-sex
sexual acts. Moreover, the country's founding president, Houphouët-Boigny, who ruled for more than three
decades, never embraced the denunciation of sexual
minorities as a political strategy.

He really had no need to, as he faced no serious
challenges to his rule or popular legitimacy. The first
decades after Côte d'Ivoire's independence in 1960 are
remembered fondly as the era of the "Ivorian Miracle,"
when high export prices for coffee and cocoa, the country's main crops, fueled staggering growth and development. The country established itself as a shining example
of post-colonial prosperity. Nowhere was this more
evident than Abidjan, which became, in the words of
the medical anthropologist Vinh-Kim Nguyen (2005),
"a self-consciously high-modern metropolis" of over
2 million people.

The bright lights of downtown came to embody the
boom, attracting migrants from throughout West Africa.
The nightlife, meanwhile, was remarkably freewheeling,
characterized by a sexual openness that extended to sexual
minorities. As the French sociologists Marc Le Pape and

Claudine Vidal (1984) have written, homosexuality was just another curiosity in a city where sexuality of all stripes was perceived "as a component of urban success."

The country's slow, painful economic decline was hastened by the collapse of commodity prices in the second half of the 1970s. Initially, though, this change had little effect on Abidjan's sexual liberalism. "Homosexuality was just not an issue in the 1970s," Nguyen says today. "It was kind of seen as part of what made Abidjan modern and interesting."

One of the main players in this early heyday for Abidjan's sexual minorities was Oscar, a hairstylist from Mali who, in 1978, organized a drag show at a Mardi Gras party. The act was such a hit that Oscar was eventually able to open a cabaret for himself and his co-stars in Zone 4, a district filled with nightclubs frequented by foreigners. The shows featured, in Nguyen's (2005) words, "brilliant impersonations of all the 'sophisticated ladies' of African cultural life"—singers, mostly—along with American stars including Diana Ross and Grace Jones, and their success generated the first local press coverage of the city's gay milieu. But while the journalists didn't shy away from the fact that Oscar and his peers slept with men, this was not the focus of their stories. "In this context, it was secondary that he [Oscar] was homosexual," Le Pape and Vidal (1984) wrote. "What was critical was that he had a sociological understanding of Ivorian high society."

The French newspaper *Libération*, in its own story on the cabaret, also made clear that fans of the performers were only mildly concerned with their sexual orientation:

> To assert that Oscar and his troupe are homosexuals is a line that most Abidjanais would not cross. Startled by the appearance and behavior of these young boys, certain would swear—often without the least proof—that we are dealing with a band of sexual inverts. We leave each side to its own truth, in order to remind the reader what is certain: we are here in the realm of art. (Mandel 1983)

Eventually, however, the realm of art succumbed to the reality of the country's economic situation. The downturn came with a host of social ramifications, including, perhaps unexpectedly, a reframing of discussions pertaining to gender and sexuality.

Vidal (1977) has chronicled how, during the boom years, Ivorian women did well for themselves in the informal sector, running ad hoc restaurants and other businesses out of their homes. When the economy faltered and men's jobs in the formal sector became more precarious, these secondary income streams became central to families' survival. As a result, the dynamic between men and women changed.

This shift generated new tensions; Vidal (1977) went so far as to describe the new gender dynamic as a "war of the sexes," noting that women were sometimes subject to violence by men looking to keep them in their place. Many Ivorian men had come to view the transformation wrought by the downturn as a threat to their time-honored position in society. The economic decline, in their minds, had precipitated a social one.

In this context, dissident forms of gender expression, which represented an even more radical departure from traditional gender roles, were seen as further signifiers of how the country was losing touch with its values. Gone were the days when Oscar's cabaret could be accepted as part of life in a modern city and discussed purely in terms of aesthetics. Instead, Oscar and his friends, whether they identified as sexual minorities or not, were subject to unprecedented levels of scrutiny. This scrutiny reflected the suspicion that such behavior might not be so harmless after all.

By the 1990s, it was becoming clear that the economic crisis would not be a mere short-term deviation from Côte d'Ivoire's post-independence success. Anxieties were heightened following the death, on December 7, 1993, of Houphouët-Boigny, who had, in the eyes of many Ivorians, saved the country from the turmoil that afflicted its neighbors. This event registered as nothing short of a national trauma. Even today, a full quarter-century later, television networks mark the anniversary of Houphouët-Boigny's death with hagiographic remembrances, and radio programs air calls from listeners describing what they were doing and how they reacted when they received the news.

The following year, in 1994, France decided to halve the value of the CFA franc, the currency backed by the French treasury that is still used in many of France's former African colonies. Though intended to spur economic growth and investment, the move came as a shock to Ivorians who, by that point, were already barely getting by. A *New York Times* story on the consequences of the devaluation described fights breaking out in markets in Abidjan and a general sense of panic. "I don't understand what the government expects us to do, where they expect us to get the money to pay when prices have doubled and our salaries remain the same," Abdou Kromah, a taxi driver with three children, was quoted as saying. "If my children get sick, am I supposed to just let them die because I don't have money for medicines? What am I supposed to do?" (Noble 1994).

As the promised benefits of the devaluation failed to materialize, suspicion mounted that ordinary Ivorians had been cheated by the country's elites. As happened in Cameroon, stories alleging that these elites engaged in same-sex sexual acts were used to set them apart from the public at large. As Nguyen (2010) writes, "Rumors of homosexuality, largely concerning shadowy figures in high places and pedophilia rings, joined the staple of sensationalist stories that also addressed witchcraft, infidelities and political corruption."

These rumors had a dampening effect on the world Brahima was just beginning to explore. By the time he met

Rodrigue in 1999, the party, as it were, seemed to be dying down, and bars like Le Dollar were relics of a scene that no longer existed.

Five months into their relationship, the party risked being shut down entirely, as the city's community of sexual minorities was shaken by the largest gay scandal in Côte d'Ivoire's history, one that, suddenly and unexpectedly, took homosexuality out of the shadows and put it at the center of public debate.

7

L'Affaire
pédophilie

These days, the building that once housed the TGV, a Lebanese-owned nightclub in the small port city of Dabou, Côte d'Ivoire, is easy to overlook. Located on the main road leading into town, some 50 kilometers west of Abidjan, its entrance is set back by a sandy walkway where young men sell airtime and women grill carp in the evenings. The wooden doors, padlocked and protected by a peach-colored iron grate, bear no markings. The space where a sign used to be is blank.

Inside, just past the doors and to the left, a drawing of a topless woman with flowing hair appears on the wall along with the words "Swing Night Club," one of several names the space was given after the TGV folded in the late 1990s. The building has been shuttered since the violence that followed Côte d'Ivoire's 2010 presidential election, however, and all the trappings of the high life are now covered in a layer of dust. Champagne flutes and wine glasses hang above the bar. Plastic champagne buckets sit on shelves in the back. Near the ceiling, above the dance floor, an air-conditioning unit dangles from the wall, suspended by a collection of cords.

Save for the dust, none of these details would be out of place in any of the nightclubs in Dabou that are currently operational. But this building is set apart by its past. Two decades ago, when it was still the TGV, it was at the center of one of the most explosive sex scandals in Ivorian history, one that extended into the ranks of the diplomatic corps as well as the highest levels of government.

The story began with a boy who, despite being just fourteen years old, was something of a fixture at the TGV, partying there until dawn many weekends. One day in 1998, this boy, identified as U.A.A. by the local press, was treated for a stomach ailment by a doctor in Dabou, according to several gay men in the city who knew him. In the course of being examined—or perhaps later, while speaking privately with relatives—U.A.A. disclosed what he believed to be the source of his illness: The owner of the nightclub, a man in his forties known as Monsieur Nabil, had forced him to engage in receptive anal sex, he said. U.A.A.'s grandmother, who looked after him, immediately notified the boy's father in Abidjan, who rushed to Dabou to file a criminal complaint.

At first, the incident attracted little attention. Though the subject matter was the type of thing that would certainly sell papers, the case involved unknown people in an out-of-the-way locale. *Soir Info*, an Abidjan-based tabloid, mentioned Nabil's arrest on its front page once in August, but paid only sporadic attention to the story after that. No other outlets picked it up.

Over the next two months, however, U.A.A.'s claims expanded. On October 5, the newspaper *Le Jour* published a front-page story with the headline "14-year-old adolescent repeatedly sodomized; prominent figures cited." In an interview with the paper, U.A.A. described how he had been assaulted by a group of men that included the Lebanese ambassador and Ezan Akélé, a member of Côte d'Ivoire's ruling party who had been serving as minister for economic infrastructure. As Vinh-Kim Nguyen notes in his account of the episode in *The Republic of Therapy: Triage and Sovereignty in West Africa's Time of AIDS* (2010), the full transcript of the interview detailed "a long and lurid tale of abduction to a karaoke club in a BMW with tinted mirrors, drugging with mysterious white powders, and subsequent sexual assault."

L'Affaire pédophilie quickly became the most talked about story in the country. In less than a month, it produced more than fifty front-page headlines in the national press. Even the state-run newspaper, *Fraternité Matin*, which was initially reluctant to pursue U.A.A.'s allegations because of their potential to damage the ruling party, eventually concluded that the scandal was too big to ignore and began covering the related court proceedings closely. October 1998, the paper declared, became Côte d'Ivoire's "month of pedophilia" (*Fraternité Matin* 1998).

Though everyone seemed to profess shock at U.A.A.'s allegations, they weren't all moved by the same details. A few of the reactions were simply homophobic. A couturier named Etienne Marcel, when asked for his thoughts on the matter by *Soir Info* (1998), said: "It's a very serious problem, because nature has made it so men should mate with women. That's what is logical."

These types of views were precisely what alarmed Brahima as he went about his life in Abidjan, watching the scandal unfold from a distance. He remembers thinking, in light of the intense interest generated by U.A.A.'s allegations, that public disdain for sexual minorities was more pervasive than he had long assumed.

Yet it appears, in retrospect, that Brahima may have misread the public mood. In reality, the response to *l'affaire pédophilie* had less to do with anti-gay sentiment than with anxieties rooted in the scandal's particular historical moment.

When *l'affaire pédophilie* exploded, Côte d'Ivoire was nearly twenty years into an economic decline that had eroded its reputation as a postcolonial success story. The death of the country's founding president, Félix Houphouët-Boigny, in 1993 had created space for a more antagonistic relationship between Ivorian citizens and their political leaders. In the popular imagination, these leaders were widely assumed to be hoarding the country's resources from the masses, and seizing the spoils for themselves. Moreover, Nguyen (2010) writes that "rumors about predatory sexual practices by powerful men worked to extend the metaphor of illicit consumption into the more charged realm of sexuality."

As discussion of alternative sexualities became increasingly bound up with the country's declining fortunes, Côte d'Ivoire adopted what Nguyen describes as a more "regressive" outlook than the one that prevailed when Abidjan's gay scene first took shape. Tolerance and even celebration of sexual minorities was replaced, in many places, with suspicion.

In this context, the specific outrage generated by *l'affaire pédophilie* was directed toward political and business elites accused of preying on defenseless children. Despite the fact that he lived fairly openly as a gay teenager, U.A.A. was portrayed not as a sexual deviant but as a sympathetic victim, even when he contradicted himself and failed to produce evidence supporting his claims. The story's gay angle was, for most people, beside the point. "This is not a banal story of homosexuality," Constance Yai Kipre Tapé, founder of the Ivorian Association in Defense of Women's Rights, told *Soir Info*. "It's time for Côte d'Ivoire to apply the law. I am worried about the trivialization of this type of violence on children."

Reflecting on the controversy, gay Ivorians say they doubt it would be met with a similar response today. In the intervening years, certain factions of Ivorian society have become increasingly concerned about the so-called importation of homosexuality from the West—one of the unintended consequences of the global LGBT rights movement's successes in other parts of the world. Were a similar scandal to unfold now, gay Ivorians say it is likely this concern would crowd out talk of predatory sexual behavior as a symptom of growing elite corruption.

To compare how *l'affaire pédophilie* was covered back in 1998 with how sexual minorities are discussed today, then, is to understand the extent to which sexual mores in Côte d'Ivoire and elsewhere in Africa are far from the timeless, immutable phenomena they are often held up to be. To the contrary, they are very much shaped by time and place.

* * *

Unlike in Abidjan, alternative sexualities were not widely discussed either directly or indirectly in Dabou in the years that preceded *l'affaire pédophilie*. This provided a kind of cover for U.A.A. to experiment with dissident forms of gender expression. Etienne, one of U.A.A.'s childhood friends and a gay man himself, says that while U.A.A. didn't cross-dress, he often wore men's clothing in an "effeminate" manner: skintight pants that showed off his backside, for example, or shirts that he tied in front, exposing his midriff. "At this time, we didn't see many homosexuals who advertised it, like we do today," Etienne recalls. This meant people were less inclined to make the link between gender nonconforming behavior and a person's sexual orientation. "If people saw you were effeminate, they wouldn't think you were homosexual."

Marc, another gay man in Dabou who was a few years younger than U.A.A. and Etienne, remembers the first time he saw U.A.A. in a school courtyard one afternoon. He was wearing short shorts and doing "the Mapouka," a slow, rhythmic, deeply sensual dance generally performed by women. "He was dancing on the field in front of his friends," Marc says. "That really attracted my attention. I said to myself, 'Who is that?'"

As it happened, U.A.A. befriended Marc's older sister and began coming by the family home. Marc marveled at U.A.A.'s ability to be "completely effeminate" in every way. "All of the elements were there," he says. "You would never know he was a man. By his voice, by his gestures, all of it." As a consequence of his appearance, U.A.A. was sometimes taunted by other boys his age, and Marc, who described his own childhood mannerisms as "naturally effeminate," eventually summoned the courage to ask him how he coped. "He said he just ignored it," Marc remembers.

He said it's his life, it's how God created him, so he can't listen to people. One time, I remember very well, I came across him in the street. I asked him what he was doing, and we stopped to talk. Some people passed us and they began to insult him. They said, "How can you dress like a woman?" They said he was cursed. He didn't even look at them.

In early 1998, U.A.A. and Etienne began going to the TGV every weekend. It was the hottest club in town then, drawing top artists from Abidjan who could usually be talked into lip-syncing a few of their hits. On weekend nights, the tiny, smoke-filled space was packed with wealthy Lebanese and Ivorians drinking liquor and champagne as they lounged on sofas or danced in front of the floor-to-ceiling mirrors that covered the walls.

The two boys would arrive sometime before midnight and stay until 4 or 5 a.m. Etienne knew U.A.A. had some sort of relationship with Monsieur Nabil, the owner, because their drinks at the TGV were always on the house. At some point in the course of most evenings, Etienne recalls, U.A.A. would leave Etienne with their other friends and climb the stairs to the second floor of the building, a private space. He would stay there for two hours or so, coming down a short while before they left for home. U.A.A. never disclosed what went on during these interludes, and Etienne says today that he never bothered to ask.

* * *

The publication of U.A.A.'s tell-all interview in *Le Jour* inflated the scandal into something the political establishment could not possibly ignore. Opposition leaders, picking up on the public's revulsion, sensed an opportunity to discredit those in power. In one article, *Notre Voie*, an opposition paper, denounced "raging" pederasty and pedophilia in Abidjan. The same article asked: "What is happening in Côte d'Ivoire so that ministers, ambassadors, whites, blacks and Arabs are free to go after the youth?"

Four days after the *Le Jour* article appeared, the government of President Henri Konan Bédié announced that, even before U.A.A.'s story had received widespread attention, four people had been arrested in connection with the allegations, charged and sent to prison. "The government understands the emotion aroused by this affair," the statement said, though it also criticized what it described as a lack of respect for the judicial process, noting that the accused were being condemned by the press before they had been tried. The statement concluded with news that the government had submitted a draft law to the National Assembly imposing harsher penalties for pedophilia and sexual harassment.

The same day this statement appeared, Ezan Akélé, the official who had been cited in the *Le Jour* article as one of U.A.A.'s assailants, read a separate statement to journalists gathered on the twenty-third floor of the Hotel Ivoire. Akélé had been removed from his ministerial post, yet the event had the feel of an official press conference.

Seated at a table with his wife and several advisers, Akélé lambasted the media storm, describing the articles as "writings worthy of the most mediocre novelists." Placing his hand on his heart, he emphasized that he was a family man, happily married with five children. "I will not tolerate even for a moment anyone to be involved in pedophilia with any member of my family," he said. He added that it was remarkable that a young boy who claimed to have been drugged could recall his alleged sexual assault with such "diabolical precision."

Homosexuality rumors had previously swirled around Akélé, though they had never received press coverage. At one point during the press conference, a journalist asked him, "Why is it always you?" Akélé said he didn't know, claimed not to have any enemies and pointed out that he had filed a defamation complaint against *Le Jour*. He said he hoped that, in the pursuit of this complaint, he might learn where the allegations originated.

The previous day, Lebanese ambassador Mohamed Daher, who had also been named by U.A.A., held a press conference of his own. "It is with much sadness that I find myself forced to react to the press campaign orchestrated against me these past few days," he said before claiming he was out of the country when U.A.A.'s assault was said to have occurred. Daher, too, attacked U.A.A.'s credibility, saying that while the teenager initially claimed to be certain the ambassador had participated in the assault, he later said only that it was someone who resembled the ambassador.

Up until that point, the press conference seemed to be going smoothly, *Soir Info* noted in its report. However, when a journalist asked Daher why he believed he had been named and not other members of the diplomatic corps, the ambassador "lost his calm." "It's a conspiracy against the Lebanese community," he insisted. "That's why I'm being targeted. The interests of the Lebanese are being targeted by another community that we don't know." A journalist then asked the ambassador whether he was gay, "causing an uproar on the part of the Lebanese present."

These statements, naturally, failed to defuse the controversy. Though it was probably necessary for Akélé and Daher to make some sort of appearance, the Ivorian public was convinced it had yet to receive the full story. Explaining why, *Soir Info*, in the confident, conversational prose of the tabloid press, evoked a separate sex scandal unfolding at around the same time on the other side of the Atlantic. "Bill Clinton energetically defended himself with his wife at his side before adopting a low profile in the Lewinsky affair, or Monicagate. This is still vivid in the minds of many Ivorians," the paper noted. "The president finally recognized that he had had improper relations with the former White House intern. Comparison without reason? In all cases, justice will take its course."

In Dabou, Marc heard of the scandal from a friend at school, and they decided to go to the courthouse on one of the days Nabil and U.A.A. were due to appear. Marc remembers that a crush of Dabou residents and journalists had gathered outside—the proceedings were closed to the public—and that many in the crowd shouted insults at Nabil as he was escorted to the entrance. "They were saying that this thing was not normal, that he had paid this child money to have sex with him," Marc says. "I remember a woman saying, 'Ah, so in this nightclub TGV, it's a pedophilia thing they are doing.'"

Many Dabou residents seemed concerned that the threat of pedophilia extended far beyond those who had been named by U.A.A., Marc says.

> I remember very well that during the scandal, my older sister said to me, "You there, you are effemi-nate. If a big person comes and approaches you and says he wants to go out with you, you need to never accept. Even if they propose money or something else, you need to never accept. If that person insists, you need to let us know."

As public anger against Nabil and his fellow defendants mounted, U.A.A.'s story began to collapse. According to media reports, the teenager ultimately accused nine people of assaulting him, seven of whom were arrested and charged. Though Akélé and Daher were never arrested or put on trial, it was Akélé's defamation case against *Le Jour* that kept the story in the headlines through the end of the year—and that ultimately exposed its significant holes.

While U.A.A. accused most of the men of assaulting him multiple times, he said he had had sex with Akélé only once. The details of this encounter seemed constantly in flux. At one point, he said it occurred on New Year's Eve 1997. At another, he cited Valentine's Day 1998. Photographic and other evidence suggested he was in Dabou both nights. Yet the three different locations he listed for the alleged encounter were in Abidjan: a karaoke bar in Plateau district, a karaoke bar in Marcory district and an Abidjan hotel.

During one court hearing in late December 1998, the director of *Le Jour* and the journalist who interviewed him said they could furnish proof that Akélé had slept with U.A.A., including graphic photos and a phone number for the minister, both provided by the teenager. But the only photo ultimately presented showed U.A.A. with friends at a party in Dabou. U.A.A. testified that he could not remember the minister's number.

These inconsistencies don't prove by any means that U.A.A. was lying. He said he had been drugged, after all, and victims of sexual assault, sober or not, can have difficulty reproducing specific details because of trauma and other factors. In the national press, however, a consensus formed that even if U.A.A. was telling the truth about Nabil and the other lesser-known defendants, he had been "manipulated" into adding Akélé and Daher to the list of accused. This was said to have happened for political reasons that were never fully explained.

Nguyen, who was in Côte d'Ivoire for the scandal, also concluded that the accusations were profoundly flawed. Though he had never met U.A.A., he noted that the teenager had a reputation among gay men for being "a twisted little queen" who was "not to be trusted," and that a prominent feminist activist who spoke with U.A.A. expressed grave doubts about his credibility. "I was left with the nagging suspicion that U.A.A.'s narrative was just a piece of gossip that had somehow gotten out of hand" (Nguyen 2010).

A court agreed with this assessment. In January 1999, Akélé won his defamation case against *Le Jour* and was awarded damages of 100,000,000 CFA francs, roughly $175,000 in current value. But gay men in Dabou hardly think this judgment is conclusive. "If it was a false accusation, it seems to me [U.A.A.] would've gone to prison for making a false accusation," Etienne says. "But he was never imprisoned. So I think he was telling the truth."

* * *

True or not, U.A.A.'s claims produced real consequences—and not just for those in power. The names of some of the most well-established families in the sizeable Lebanese community were irrevocably damaged. At the height of the scandal, in mid-October, *Soir Info* reported that a Lebanese woman in Dabou named Zakiah Zabad, whose son, nephew and brother-in-law were all implicated, suffered a heart attack while arrests were being carried out. "My family is a very religious family," Yamad Zabad, another son of the woman, told the paper. "And since we have been in Dabou for 20 years, we have never had any involvement with the police or the gendarmerie. My mother, learning of these lies, could not bear it. She had a heart attack and fell into a coma in the presence of police." She died soon after at an Abidjan hospital.

The scandal was also blamed for costing the life of a Frenchman who was well-known in the local gay community. This man was among the seven who were arrested as a result of U.A.A.'s allegations. While his family was able to secure his release, he died of an illness that friends said he contracted while incarcerated.

For others, the scandal blew over almost as quickly as it had emerged. "People spoke about it, but it was not something that made them act crazy, no," Etienne says. "People said, 'Hey, the nightclub is like that. It's a nightclub for homosexuals. Everything was hidden from us.' And then everyone forgot about it."

All of the arrested men were eventually released. Nabil left town temporarily, though he later returned to Dabou. He lost his nightclub but continued to work at a hardware store he owned. He died in town a few years ago.

For his part, U.A.A. quickly disappeared. Rumors circulated that his family had sent him to Europe to ensure his safety, though he was later believed to be back in Abidjan. His whereabouts today are a mystery.

Marc, who as a young teenager behaved like U.A.A. in many ways, later adopted more "masculine" mannerisms, though he says this wasn't a direct result of the scandal. Even before *l'affaire pédophilie*, his older brothers were trying to get him to change his ways—encouraging him to play sports and, one time, burning a doll he had purchased with his pocket money. "The only person who supported me a bit was my mom," Marc says, describing his adolescence. "She said, 'He's been like that since he was a child. If he needs to change, it's God who will decide.' She always said that, even to my father."

When he was younger, Marc had one friend who shared some of his "effeminate" traits. They walked and talked "like girls," Marc said, and sometimes wore girls' clothing. When this friend moved away in 2001, Marc felt abandoned and decided to conform to his brothers' idea of what was normal. He started playing soccer. He lowered the tone of his voice. He spent hours in front of the mirror trying to alter his hand gestures, jamming his hands in his pockets, for example, instead of resting them on his hips. He was ultimately so successful that, a few years ago, when he ran into Etienne in Abidjan after the two hadn't seen each other for a while, Etienne was stunned by the change. "He kept asking me, 'How did you do that? How did you do that? Explain,'" Marc said.

Today, Marc is glad he underwent this transformation. In recent years, he says, as awareness of homosexuality has increased in Côte d'Ivoire, the population has become wary of "effeminate" men who, in an earlier time, might have gone through life relatively unnoticed. If he acted today as he did as a child, he would probably be forced to stay in Dabou among people who had grown accustomed to his behavior when he was small. He would never have been able to set out on his own and make a life for himself in Abidjan.

"A lot of things have changed. People have become more intolerant," Marc says. He recalls how, in 2014, following an attack on the Abidjan headquarters of Côte d'Ivoire's most prominent LGBT rights organization, an imam at the biggest mosque in Dabou warned worshipers that gay people were keen on "invading" the town. Talk like this, Marc says, proves that life has become more difficult for Ivorian sexual minorities since 1998.

If such views had prevailed at the time, Marc believes the entire conversation around *l'affaire pédophilie* would have unfolded differently. In particular, he thinks that U.A.A., because of his mannerisms and his reputation for flaunting gender conventions, would have come in for much harsher treatment. "They would say he provoked them by acting effeminate," Marc says. "If the scandal happened today, everyone would blame him, the victim."

8

A life
for two

L'Affaire pédophilie turned out to be a major turning point for Brahima. The incident compounded his already significant insecurities about being a man who dated and slept with other men. Ivorians' fascination with what may or may not have happened on the second floor of the TGV pointed to widespread homophobia, he says, and "permitted you to see who people really were." Long before the scandal wrapped up, he'd decided to cut ties with the city's gay milieu altogether and resume dating women.

"In Côte d'Ivoire, there is a problem," he explains. "If you are homosexual, it touches everyone. It touches your whole family. People will insult you, they'll insult your children, insult your name. Me, to preserve my name for my children, I need to do it in discretion." He broke off his relationship with Rodrigue, the man he had been dating at the time. As was the case with Woulai Bah, his first boyfriend, he never saw Rodrigue again.

For Muriel, the woman who would become Brahima's next lover and partner, *l'affaire pédophilie* was similarly disruptive. She had been living in Dabou for a few years when the story broke, studying at a high school there and taking full advantage of her first long stay away from her family back in Douala. Drawn in by Ivorian nightlife, which she described as "impeccable" even in a small port town, she had grown accustomed to spending weekend nights dancing and drinking at the TGV.

She remembers that the scandal hit Dabou "like a bomb." She had dated two business partners of Monsieur Nabil, the TGV's owner, and she considered him a friend, someone who was "really nice" and harmless. The fact that the whole country turned against him so quickly frightened her, as did the broader anti-Lebanese rhetoric U.A.A.'s allegations inspired—rhetoric that she feared could, under different circumstances, be directed toward her, another foreigner. "The city became a bit bizarre. People became reticent, they were no longer jovial," she says. "A lot of people left Dabou. It was already a small city, but it became even smaller." She decided to abandon her studies and leave as well.

She moved in with her older sister, Yolande, who had also relocated from Cameroon to Côte d'Ivoire and was living in an apartment complex in Abidjan's Adjamé district known as 220 Logements. As it happened, the apartment was down the hall from Brahima, who at the time was making good money selling motorcycle parts upcountry. It did not take Muriel long to notice the neighbor with the seemingly endless supply of fresh jerseys, polos, sneakers and jeans. "Ivorians know how to dress," Muriel says. "When you see an Ivorian man in front of you, you can think it's a man from the West."

Brahima had other qualities that appealed to her as well. "What I liked most about him is that he really liked *le partage*," she says, referring to his habit of sharing whatever he had with friends in the neighborhood, inviting them out and paying for their one-liter bottles of Bock beer. "He brought people together. He really liked to dialogue. He was amusing. And that really made a mark on me."

Muriel had the good fortune of meeting Brahima during what he now refers to as the happiest time of his life. He was the wealthiest he'd ever been. In the early 2000s, he says, taxis were not as common as they are today in cities and towns outside of Abidjan, so many Ivorians who could not afford cars of their own depended on motorcycles, and moto-taxis, to get around. Brahima's boss, a Lebanese businessman, had cornered a large section of the market for spare motorcycle parts, and he paid handsome salaries to Brahima and the other salesmen. It was one of the few periods of Brahima's life when he wanted for nothing.

Côte d'Ivoire had experienced a coup in 1999 and spent much of 2000 under military rule. Even after Laurent

Gbagbo, a former professor, came to power that October, the country's economic slump continued, meaning Brahima's success set him apart from many men his age. "I had my house, I was all set up," he says. "All the women wanted to come back to my room."

To get his attention, Muriel made the first move one day after Brahima returned from work. "It's a day I remember very well," Brahima says. On the way home, he'd stopped by City Sport to buy a new pair of sneakers that would better match the jersey he was wearing, that of the Ukrainian soccer star Andriy Shevchenko, who was then playing for AC Milan. When he got to 220 Logements, he chatted a bit with a friend of Yolande's, then showered and got ready to go out. As he was leaving, Muriel called over to ask why he hadn't invited her to join. "And I said, 'I'm sorry, I didn't know that I was supposed to invite you,'" Brahima recalls. "'But it doesn't bother me at all if you want to come.'" They spent the first of many nights in plastic chairs around a table at an open-air maquis. "We got there and he called his friends," Muriel says. "We ate, we drank, we discussed."

For a while, the two kept their relationship hidden from everyone but Muriel's sister. Muriel would spend the night at Brahima's, then wake up at 4 a.m. and scurry down the hall to Yolande's place so the neighbors wouldn't find out. They became more open and serious after Muriel accepted Brahima's invitation to move in with him. In early 2002, when Muriel's father died, Brahima paid for the plane ticket so she could go home to bury him. But she returned to Abidjan immediately, resisting her family's entreaties to stay.

The life they had made in Abidjan, though, was soon to unravel. Business for Brahima, which had already started to slow down, suffered a crushing blow when northern rebel groups attempted another coup in September 2002. Gbagbo managed to stay on as president, but the northern half of the country fell under rebel control, meaning Brahima could no longer work as he had before.

One month before this latest round of unrest, Muriel had given birth to their first child, a girl named Audrey, named after Muriel's mother. The instability convinced Muriel it was time to return home, and Brahima decided to accompany her. It was important to both of them that Muriel's family know she had not fallen in with "a bad guy." Brahima had also started thinking about making his way to the United States, and a cousin advised him that, given Côte d'Ivoire's political troubles, it might be easier to sort the papers with the US Embassy in Cameroon. On November 16, 2002, they boarded an evening flight out of Abidjan, Brahima's first.

Brahima knew very little about his new home. Muriel had talked a few times about *ndolé*, the bitter stew that is a national staple, though he had never tasted it. His general view of Cameroon was shaped, apart from his relationship with Muriel, by the Indomitable Lions, the national soccer team that had won the previous two Africa Cup of Nations titles. The team's success, he says, lent a certain caché to associations with Cameroonians, especially romantic ones. "It was something I took pride in, as an Ivorian, to have met a Cameroonian girl," Brahima says. "It was the wish of all Ivorian men at the time to meet a Cameroonian girl."

Yet soccer prowess is a poor barometer for development, and Brahima was disappointed by what he found when he arrived in Cameroon. "It was supposed to be a modern country, but it wasn't a beautiful country like Côte d'Ivoire," he says. "Côte d'Ivoire is more developed, you can have roads. Even the road between Douala and Yaoundé, it wasn't even a highway."

The main letdown, though, was Brahima's inability to land steady work. He found the business world ethnically balkanized and hostile to foreigners, and while he didn't necessarily need the money—he had saved quite a bit in Abidjan, and Muriel was helping to manage a popular nightclub started by her father—his newfound idleness clashed with the identity he'd worked hard to build for himself. It also altered the dynamic of his relationship with Muriel, for whom he'd once been a provider.

He soon began spending more time drinking, a pastime he'd picked up after the death of his mother in 2000. "Sometimes it was difficult for Brahima here," says Cyriel, a hairstylist from Douala who became a close friend. "He wanted to stabilize himself, but he wasn't succeeding." With increasing frequency, Brahima passed his days at the bar near Cyriel's salon, drinking 33, the local beer, by himself, having only Cyriel to talk to when the latter went on break. Then he and Cyriel would hit the bars, but Brahima's inability to handle his alcohol meant their nights out often became drama-filled.

"He wasn't an alcoholic," Cyriel says. "When he was in his element, surrounded by people he liked and who understood him, he could have a very good time." But Brahima could also become aggressive, and at least once Cyriel had to drag him out of a bar to avoid a brawl. Muriel says Brahima was notorious for picking fights if he was out too long. "The only thing with Brahima is that when he has one drink too many," she says, "it's a catastrophe."

Back at home with her family, Muriel sought a calmer life than the one they'd had in Abidjan. Brahima, however, seemed to want to go out more and more. "The problem was that he went out too much," Muriel says. "I didn't appreciate it. He had too many friends, company that I didn't like. My life in Abidjan and my life here were different."

Brahima acknowledges today that he disappointed Muriel, though he suspects his unemployment was a bigger factor in their breakup than his partying. "When we are young, we think that everyone who wears a nice shirt and nice pants can make a life for us," he says, explaining why he thinks Muriel was first drawn to him. "That's when we're small. When we grow up, we learn that it doesn't always work out. She had wanted to make her life with me. But when she noticed that things with me weren't always

147

going to be ideal, she wanted me to give her a bit more money, all of that..." The strain on the relationship, he says, ultimately proved too much.

Their official split was brought about by Brahima's affair with Jeannette, a much older woman in the neighborhood—someone Muriel says "had watched me grow up." When neighbors started asking Muriel whether Brahima and Jeannette were sleeping together, she became enraged and called Jeannette directly. Jeannette reported Muriel to the military police, saying Muriel had threatened to kill her, and all three of them were briefly detained.

Brahima recognized even then that he was in the wrong. "If there's anybody who is guilty, it is me," he says. But instead of trying to reconcile with Muriel, Brahima did what he'd gotten in the habit of doing when he became unsure about a relationship: He left. First he moved to his own apartment. Then, without telling anyone of his plans, he left Douala altogether shortly after New Year's Day 2005, setting out for a new life in Yaoundé.

* * *

Brahima's stretch of good luck had ended abruptly. Just a few years earlier, before he left Côte d'Ivoire for Cameroon, he had attained the touchstones of the adult life he'd long wanted: independence, financial security and a partner with whom he could form a family. By the time he reached Yaoundé, however, his savings were fast disappearing and he was alone and disheartened.

It is likely impossible even for Brahima to pinpoint all the causes of this fall, much less rank them in order of importance. Along with the obvious ones—his money troubles, the mess resulting from his infidelity—there were others that may have been just as decisive. Perhaps he had lost interest in Muriel. Perhaps he simply wanted out of Douala. Or perhaps Brahima hoped to continue acting on his attraction to men.

There is some evidence this last temptation was playing on Brahima's mind. His relationship with Cyriel, the hairstylist, sat close to the line between friendship and romance. They spoke every day, went to bars together many evenings and sometimes ended up at Cyriel's apartment, where they shared a bed. But Cyriel, who has long been openly gay, says they mostly flirted, and that their physical intimacy never extended beyond holding each other at night. Brahima says he would never have felt comfortable conducting affairs with men in Douala for fear that word might get back to Muriel and her relatives. In Yaoundé, though, he had no strong connections and therefore no such concerns. "When I was in Douala, I suffered," Brahima says. "But when I got to Yaoundé, I broke out."

His first contact in Yaoundé was an Ivorian man named Traoré, who worked in the city as a tailor. Traoré housed him for two days, then helped him find a cheap hotel where he could stay while looking for something more permanent. It was at a maquis next to Traoré's workspace where

Brahima was introduced to Thierry, the man who would offer him long-term lodging and, in short order, become his next boyfriend.

Thierry, who was around twenty-five at the time, lived on his family's compound in the Yaoundé neighborhood known as Briqueterie. His father, a retired police officer, had upwards of ten children from two wives. In addition to this large immediate family, Thierry grew up surrounded by aunts, cousins, nieces and nephews. But the chaos of the place suited him. He also had his own room where he could go when he needed time to himself.

Whereas Brahima describes having been "initiated" into homosexuality by his first lovers, Thierry is convinced he was destined to be gay long before he knew what sexuality was. As a young boy, he rarely left his mother's side, accompanying her to the market and assisting her in the kitchen. When he wasn't doing that, he played with dolls alongside the young girls in his family and tried not to so much as touch a soccer ball if he could help it.

At around age fourteen, Thierry realized he was attracted to one of his uncles, Blaise, a younger brother of his mother. He would catch himself stealing glances at Blaise's body as he stepped out of the shower. When Blaise's girlfriends came by the house, Thierry would run away, doing whatever he could to avoid the image of his uncle with a woman.

Thierry got the message early on that his behavior, and his feelings, were abnormal. Relatives would tease him and sometimes hit him for preferring the company of girls. His attraction for Blaise was more confusing than anything else, but he knew that he should try to stifle it, and he went to the Catholic church his family attended to pray for help in doing so. "I was certain that I was the only person who was like this," he says, "because I had never met anyone who had these attitudes, and no one ever spoke about it." At the same time, his parents never came down too hard on him, instead giving him space to explore who he was.

His first chance to act on his attraction to men came thanks to an older cousin named Sophie, who worked at Yaoundé's Hotel Mont Fébé and spent her free time chasing after its foreign, mainly white, clients. For several months, Sophie dated an Australian man named Ken who frequented the hotel and took her out to restaurants and clubs when she wasn't working. What Thierry didn't realize was that Ken and Sophie had never actually slept together. Sophie puzzled over this until the day she introduced Ken to Thierry. From that point on, Ken created space for Thierry in the relationship; when he gave Sophie money, he gave Thierry the same amount, and Thierry was soon invited wherever they went.

Sophie soon told Thierry of her suspicion that Ken was in love with him. Thierry feigned both disgust and ignorance, saying he did not understand how a man could be attracted to another man. "But at the bottom of my heart, I was very happy to hear it," he says. "I said to myself, 'That really exists. I'm not alone.'" Nevertheless, he resisted. "Don't talk to me about that. It's horrible," he remembers saying. Sophie responded: "If he hits on you, you need to accept. Look, he takes good care of us. He's enabled us to have a bit of well-being. If he's interested in you, what's the problem?"

Thierry went home as excited as he'd ever been. "I can't tell you how happy I was," he says. "I only had one wish, which was to see him." Yet he knew Ken would have to initiate anything remotely romantic or sexual, as Thierry wouldn't have the nerve to do so himself.

Ken did not keep him waiting. Encouraged by Sophie, he invited Thierry for a night out, just the two of them. Over dinner, he probed for details of Thierry's personal life: "Do you have a girlfriend? Do you make love to her?" Later, driving back after a night out dancing, Ken said it made more sense for Thierry to sleep at his house, offering the weak explanation that Thierry's neighborhood was too "dangerous" for him to drive in. Thierry happily agreed, though he had no idea what was about to happen, or what sex between men even looked like. "I kept thinking, 'How will it work?'"

Once they got through the door, Ken went to take a shower. When he got out, he walked over to Thierry, pushed him up against the wall and kissed him. Thierry says he had an instant orgasm, and then began to cry. "It was very strong, I assure you," he says.

They didn't have sex that night, but they were inseparable for the rest of Ken's stay in Cameroon. Ken even brought up the idea of taking Thierry back to Australia with him, but Thierry, who had rarely left Yaoundé, never took this seriously. "I was afraid to travel that far," he says. "There was also a lot of discussion at the time in Cameroon around white men being gay and taking Cameroonians with them to Europe, so there would have been some stigma." He believes, though, that other members of his family besides Sophie understood the nature of his relationship with Ken, and simply chose not to discuss it.

After Ken left, Thierry continued to date men, primarily Europeans. He still socialized chiefly with women and helped his mother around the house, but his family paid him little mind, even when he dyed his hair beige or khaki. Then, one day, his younger brother found a phone with photos of Thierry and one of his white boyfriends.

This brother was a regular source of anxiety for their parents, who had been forced, on multiple occasions, to pay for his release from the local police station for theft and other petty crimes. Jealous of Thierry's status as a family favorite, he presented the photos to their parents one day as proof that Thierry was a worthless "*pédé*." In response, Thierry's father said, "I'd prefer 100 times over to have a son who's a *pédé* than to have a bandit like you." That was the closest Thierry came to knowing what his father thought about his sexuality; the subject never came up again.

Thierry also slept with women from time to time, and he fathered a child with a female friend of his, giving his parents a grandchild to care for. His position in the family was thus more than secure by the time Brahima came into his life.

* * *

Hearing Brahima and Thierry talk about their relationship, one comes away with the sense that it was more a set of shared circumstances than a shared experience. They agree on the broad contours, and many details, of their time together, but their accounts diverge in important ways, creating a record of disconnect.

Brahima describes an uncomplicated beginning. Immediately upon their first meeting, he says, Thierry's attentive, caring manner called to mind Woulai Bah and Rodrigue. Just like these early boyfriends, Thierry "does everything to put you at ease," Brahima says. When Thierry heard Brahima was low on cash, he immediately offered to house him even though they barely knew each other. Brahima says they started dating almost immediately after he moved in.

Thierry's recollection is fuller, and messier. Like Muriel, he was attracted to Brahima from the beginning, drawn in by his looks and especially his clothing. At the time, Cameroonian men tended to wear shirts that were large and baggy. Brahima's shirts, by contrast, clung tightly to his body and were well-ironed, with every button in place. "It was very beautiful to see," Thierry says. Yet despite their mutual attraction, he says the two men did not embark on a relationship right away, as Brahima claims. That's because Brahima was dating Thierry's cousin, Aline.

For the first weeks of their time together, Thierry says, Aline was always around, and the group would go out as a threesome. Because Aline lived in a single room with her mother and little sister, and because Brahima had limited funds with which to pay for a hotel, they often ended up back at Thierry's place. Though Thierry happily extended these invitations, insisting they all sleep on the same bed, this meant he was forced to lie there and listen as Brahima and Aline had sex. "I was very much not at ease," he says, laughing at the memory. "I acted like I didn't hear anything, but I heard everything. I wanted to be in the place of my cousin."

He soon got his wish. One night, Brahima and Aline went out without Thierry, but Brahima returned alone at 3 a.m., visibly drunk. As Thierry remembers it, the two men had sex "without posing any questions," as if it were the most natural thing in the world. "He climbed on top of me, and I was very happy," Thierry says. "We didn't have condoms, we didn't have lubricant. There was nothing at the house. We just made love like that." It was the first time Thierry had assumed the receptive role in anal sex. Though he was in pain the next day, Brahima assured him it would pass, and eventually it did. They began sleeping together on a regular basis, and Brahima became a full-time guest at the house, a situation that lasted until he left the country.

It was the first time Brahima had lived with a man he was dating, and he drew inspiration from just how little Thierry seemed to care for what other people thought. "Me, I liked to make a show by walking around with a woman on my arm, to hide myself. He was more open," Brahima recalls. Before long, Brahima had no problem spending all his time with Thierry even though most people seemed to know Thierry was gay. "I didn't care," Brahima says.

Because neither of them worked, they spent long days in Thierry's room watching television, reading the papers and chatting with friends of Thierry's who stopped by. For Brahima, the room became a kind of sanctuary, free of the tension that had spoiled his time in Douala. "I had just gotten away from these stories of women, all these stories of Douala, where women are doing things behind the scenes, the strong jealousy of Muriel, all of that," he says. At Thierry's house, by contrast, "It was total freedom."

Their relative isolation from the rest of the world permitted them to become fully immersed in their relationship with each other. "We slept together, we shared certain experiences—how we came to know certain things, how we became gay, our feelings, how we saw other gays, their behavior, their attitudes," Brahima says. "The most important experience was passing time together, sleeping together when we wanted to, living our life like we wanted to together, without pressure... All the moments of this time were good."

Thierry remembers all this differently. For one thing, Brahima's moods were volatile, largely because he remained unable to control his drinking. When they went out, the bar crowds in Yaoundé frequently warmed to his sense of fashion, Ivorian accent and ability to break down the Ivorian street slang, known as nouchi, that peppered the songs by Abidjan bands like Espoir 2000 and Garagistes that were so popular at the time. Yet things could go south quickly. "Nights could pass very badly with him," Thierry remembers, "because when he drank a bit of alcohol, he began to have a very nasty tongue." He would insult the very people who had been his friends moments before, and sometimes extend his ire to the country where he was trying to make a new life for himself, calling Cameroonians "villagers" who dressed poorly.

Life at the house was also mixed. Thierry relished the experience of dating a fellow African, someone he had far more in common with than his previous Western boyfriends. "For me, it was a bit like a mystery to go out with a black like me, to make love with a black like me," he says. "For me it was something that I wanted to discover." When money was low, Brahima hardly left the house for weeks at a time, and the pair settled into a highly routinized domestic life, with Thierry preparing meals of meat or fish with rice or attiéké, an Ivorian staple made of fermented cassava pounded into a kind of couscous.

Brahima treated Thierry's parents respectfully, but he didn't like to spend much time around them, meaning their entire existence was confined to Thierry's room, whose furnishings were limited to the bed and a small armoire for their clothes and other belongings. Brahima didn't have much, and he was possessive over his clothes in particular. There was only one item he ever permitted Thierry to wear: a red T-shirt with the name of the Italian designer Gianfranco Ferré written across the chest.

For Thierry, the emotional connection was less involved than what Brahima described. "There wasn't much tenderness. We stayed at the house like buddies, like friends," he says. There was no real intimacy, no stolen kisses, no falling asleep in one another's arms. "We only had this tenderness when we were making love," he says. "Afterwards, we went back to our corners."

Though Thierry clearly wanted more, he hesitated to make any demands of Brahima, fearing he would scare him off. The result was that Brahima was in charge of the relationship, controlling when they had sex and even when they spoke. "I didn't look for more than what he gave me," Thierry says.

* * *

Their emotional distance notwithstanding, Thierry understood that Brahima remained distraught over his inability to find work, and sometimes encouraged him to get out of the house instead of sulking. Whenever either of them had a bit of extra money, they would head to the casino, or to the few bars in Yaoundé that had a reputation for being gay-friendly. Brahima didn't stay long enough in Yaoundé to feel like he was part of this scene, but he respected how the city's gay men "lived their passion" in a "well-organized" way, by which he means how they discreetly created space for themselves even during a period marred by intensifying homophobia.

These nights did little to alleviate the dark moods stemming from his poor finances and lack of plan for the future. "I often asked myself what I was doing in this country," Brahima says. At those times, he adds, "Everyone around me bothered me."

He talked about trying to go to Europe, and he would sometimes call an Ivorian friend, a soccer player, who had established himself in France. This man, Thierry says, would sometimes send Brahima money, offering a temporary reprieve from his inability to do much of anything in Cameroon, as well as from the depressing notion that he was stuck there, unable to afford the trip home.

More often, though, Brahima reminisced about his life in Adjamé, just before he met Muriel. He described the money he was able to earn before Côte d'Ivoire descended into conflict, and the friends with whom he'd spent it. "I ended up learning a lot about this neighborhood," Thierry says of Adjamé, "as though I myself had lived there."

As Brahima's savings continued to evaporate, he grew more worried. The friends and relatives in Côte d'Ivoire and elsewhere who had periodically sent him loans became increasingly reluctant to take his calls. Life with Thierry was also beginning to sour, again largely because of Brahima's behavior. They were spending less time together, as Brahima had begun dating a new woman. Thierry doesn't remember what this woman did to earn money, but she seemed to have more than enough of it, something Brahima benefited from during the brief time they were together, enjoying the nights out he had once been able to finance on his own. When that relationship ended, Brahima resumed dating Aline, Thierry's cousin. Though Brahima and Thierry still slept together frequently, Thierry once again found himself cast out from the center of Brahima's life, forced to compete for his attention.

Finally, toward the end of 2005, Brahima concluded that life in Cameroon was untenable. He convinced his brother to send money for the overland journey back to Côte d'Ivoire, then broke the news to Thierry that he would soon be gone.

Thierry had seen this coming. Nevertheless, their split was drawn out and painful. In the weeks leading up to Brahima's departure, Thierry wanted to sleep with him as much as possible, to experience what tenderness he could before it was gone forever. But Brahima, still dating Aline, was preoccupied, and their time together was more limited than ever before. "I didn't cry in front of Brahima, but I cried a lot in those days," Thierry remembers. "I was very much in love with him, despite his behavior."

The plan was for Aline to accompany Brahima to Douala, where he would begin his return trip alone by bus and shared taxi, hugging the coast of the Gulf of Guinea until he reached Ivorian soil. Thierry went with them to the bus station in Yaoundé, where the two men shared an awkward goodbye as Aline looked on. But Thierry wasn't satisfied; he couldn't accept that the man he'd lived with for months was, just like that, out of his life. After the bus ferrying Brahima and Aline to Douala left the station, he paid for a seat in a car and followed them, meaning they would all spend Brahima's last days in Cameroon together.

To this day, Thierry is grateful he did this. Though Aline's presence meant he wouldn't be able to sleep with Brahima one last time, their time in Douala offered some confirmation that what they'd shared was real, and that Brahima, though he didn't always show it, was sad they were parting ways. Brahima was on his best behavior, treating Thierry and Aline with the courtesy that, under normal conditions, he so often lacked. "He didn't insult us anymore," Thierry says. "He wasn't wicked anymore. He was more tender with me during this period, I believe."

Their last night together, dinner and drinks before retiring early so Brahima could get on the road the next morning, was a somber affair. "He was calmer than usual, and he didn't speak a lot," Thierry says of Brahima.

I had only one wish: to take him in my arms. But when we said goodbye, it was like we normally did: "Take care of yourself, send me your news." That really hurt me, because I shouldn't have said goodbye to someone like him in this manner. I wanted to take him in my arms, to hold him tight, but I couldn't. I had to contain myself.

Brahima, too, kept his feelings to himself, leaving Thierry to guess what was in his head. "I think he was feeling worse than me because he didn't look at me," Thierry says. "He spoke the whole time with his head lowered. I think that in his head he was already reflecting. I don't know about what."

At first, Thierry doubted whether Brahima would actually leave Cameroon. But Brahima called him several times from the road, and Thierry got the confirmation he needed when the country code was no longer Cameroon's +237. Though he expected the calls would continue, they stopped after Brahima reached Côte d'Ivoire. Brahima says he couldn't afford the phone credit, and that, in any case, he was too busy trying to build a new life for himself in his home city.

Brahima would nevertheless remain on Thierry's mind, and weigh on his heart, long after they said goodbye. As a parting gift, he had left Thierry the red Gianfranco Ferré T-shirt he loved, and Thierry wore it to pieces. He realized he would need to start dating again if he wanted to move on. "I began thinking, 'I need to find my other Brahima,'" he says.

Despite his concerns about safety, he began seeking out gay-friendly bars in Yaoundé, and also meeting guys online.

One of them, a Swiss national posted to the embassy in Yaoundé, eventually helped him sort his papers so he could travel to Europe. Like many sexual minorities in Cameroon and throughout the region, Thierry had convinced himself that only by leaving Africa would he be able to live openly as himself.

When Thierry told his family of his plans, they were supportive. His mother, with whom he had always been close, indicated that she fully understood his motivations. "It's after some time that I understood everything she was saying," he recalls. "She said, 'Thierry, I'm happy for you, because there, you will be able to live your life freely, without bothering anyone.'" That was as close as they ever came to discussing his homosexuality.

Thierry found himself thinking about Brahima a few years later, when he first went to Paris. For all he knew, Brahima had connected with the Ivorians he knew in the city and moved there himself. On the Champs Elysées, he went to the Gianfranco Ferré boutique and bought a shirt to replace the one Brahima had left him. He continues to think of Brahima, more than his earlier, white boyfriends, as the *déclic* that brought his life into focus, the person who set him down a path of living openly as a gay man.

But the two men never again reunited, and Thierry regrets that they never had a chance to seriously discuss their relationship and what they meant to each other. "I regret that at the time he didn't speak a lot about his sexuality, that he was so hidden," Thierry says. "Because

I was discovering things and I would have loved to have someone who understood, and who could've explained things to me. Brahima always went out with me like I was the first and the only man that he knew. I regret that today, because I think he had relations with men before, and he knew a lot of things he could have explained to me, but he never talked to me about them."

Brahima also remembers the relationship fondly. Though he says he was too distracted by the question of how to get his life back on track to have fallen fully in love with Thierry, he looks back on their relationship "with strong feelings" and appreciates everything Therry tried to do for him.

"We lived it. It was a life for two," Brahima says. "And there was a lot of encouragement. Despite the problems, it was a good time. Compared to the other times, it was a good time. That's all."

9

Winners
and losers

Brahima arrived in his hometown convinced his most aimless days were behind him. "I had a clear objective," he says. "It was to begin again. I didn't have anything anymore. I didn't have a job, I didn't have activities. I didn't even have a house."

What he did have was an unshakeable belief that he would be able to turn his life around. Throughout his stay in Cameroon, he had clung to memories of Abidjan as a place where good, even great things could happen. It was a city that, unlike Douala or Yaoundé, had rewarded his energy and entrepreneurship, enabling him to construct a comfortable life for himself in the years before he met Muriel and moved away. Though the city had no doubt changed since then, and he didn't know what those changes would mean for him personally, even this uncertainty was a welcome novelty. In Cameroon, he had been worn down by the feeling that he could stay forever and it wouldn't matter. The political and economic situation would remain stuck, and he would remain stuck, too.

He acknowledges today that, given how high his expectations were, some disappointment was probably inevitable. Yet the reality of what he encountered back home was demoralizing in ways he didn't expect. As he settled in, Brahima realized that the city had an altogether different feel from when he'd last lived there—one that was uncomfortably reminiscent of the stagnation he'd been yearning to escape.

In November 2002, when Brahima and Muriel had moved to Douala, Côte d'Ivoire was still processing the coup attempt against then-President Laurent Gbagbo. The rebels, who had failed to take Abidjan, were working to consolidate control of the northern cities of Korhogo and Bouaké, the latter of which would become their capital. The whole situation still seemed somewhat fluid.

By the time Brahima came back, Côte d'Ivoire had become trapped somewhere between peace and conflict, with no obvious way out. In 2003, United Nations peace-keepers had established a buffer zone between the rebel-held north and the Gbagbo-controlled south, splitting the country in two.

This division would hold until 2007, when the government and the rebels signed a peace deal and the buffer zone was dismantled. Even with this breakthrough, it would take three more years before Côte d'Ivoire organized new elections. The lack of a clear path forward stifled growth and investment, limiting the opportunities Brahima needed to reinvent himself.

* * *

This national holding pattern did not mean, however, that all aspects of Ivorian life remained frozen. For Côte d'Ivoire's sexual minorities, the first decade of the twenty-first century was a time of profound upheaval. As they grappled with the aftermath of *l'affaire pédophilie* and the challenges that followed, a nascent network of activists tested responses to their changing circumstances, charting new paths for how to talk about themselves and how to take up space in the world.

Traditionally, associating with Côte d'Ivoire's gay scene—whether by simply going to parties or actually engaging in same-sex sexual acts—has not required making any kind of definitive statement about one's identity. This is apparent in the words Ivorian sexual minorities use to refer to themselves and to one another. Rather than "gay" or "homosexual"—which invoke something innate and immutable about the person being described—it has been more common to employ words like *branché*, which is French slang for "plugged in" or "trendy." In part, such language is a tool for speaking discreetly. But it also suggests an element of fluidity, or slipperiness, that is similarly reflected in how members of the scene describe their introductions to it; as Nguyen notes in *The Republic of Therapy* (2010), a common formulation, *on m'a mis dedans*, is decidedly passive. In English, it translates as, "Someone got me into it."

The anthropologist Matthew Thomann (2014) has written about how, over time, Ivorians who belonged to the scene developed a coded language, known as *woubi-can*, to describe some of its racier aspects; *woubi-can* words cover topics like sexual acts, sexual positions and penis size. Two of the most important *woubi-can* words are used to talk about the highly gendered relationships typical of Ivorian men who have sex with men. The first, y*ossi*, refers to the partner who "plays the role of the man" in everything from household duties to anal sex. His *woubi*, by contrast, "plays the role of the woman," often cooking and cleaning and, in the bedroom, acting as the receptive sexual partner. These terms can be assumed as identities, and they often are. Fundamentally, though, they are rooted in behaviors. At least theoretically, it is easier to imagine someone ceasing to be a *yossi* or a *woubi*—or ceasing to be *branché*—than it is to imagine someone ceasing to be gay.

Beginning in the 1990s, several factors had the effect of blurring, at least partially, this distinction between behavior and identity. First, depictions of alternative sexualities in the Ivorian press, with their tendency to fix their subjects in place, did not customarily allow for this kind of nuance. In such accounts, men and women who engaged in same-sex sexual acts did so because that was who they *were*, end of discussion.

The arrival of HIV/AIDS in West Africa would prove even more consequential. By 1994, the disease had become the leading cause of death in Abidjan, and Côte d'Ivoire had emerged as the epicenter of the epidemic for the region. As Nguyen (2010) writes, international development organizations began desperately looking for HIV-positive West Africans who could spread the word about the importance of prevention, testing and treatment. First-person testimonials, to be used in public awareness campaigns, became highly valuable, and could be converted into material benefits for those who provided them. These benefits included trips to conferences overseas and access to antiretroviral drugs. At a time when these medications were not yet widely available on the continent, a willingness to "come out" as HIV-positive therefore represented a way for West Africans to save their own lives.

For a number of reasons, Ivorian men who have sex with men played central roles in the civil society movement that formed to represent the interests of people living with HIV/AIDS. For one thing, such men were heavily affected by the epidemic. Additionally, HIV/AIDS activism gave them new opportunities to come together at a time when their previous gathering spaces—namely, friendly bars and nightclubs—were increasingly under threat.

By becoming intimately involved in this movement, these men were able to see firsthand the benefits of finding common cause with foreign governments and other entities, which had resources far surpassing anything they could access at home. Crucially, this important lesson was imparted just as those resources were about to expand.

In 2003, US President George W. Bush established PEPFAR, the President's Emergency Plan for AIDS Relief. In his State of the Union address that year, drawing upon the language of compassionate conservatism, Bush described it as "a work of mercy beyond all current international efforts to help the people of Africa." Côte d'Ivoire was among the first countries to receive funding, meaning PEPFAR instantly became a major player among public health donors, pumping hundreds of millions of dollars into the sector.

The influx of cash greatly deepened exchanges between Ivorian sexual minority activists and outside forces. PEPFAR selected the Chicago-based organization Heartland Alliance International as one of its implementing partners, and Heartland in turn contracted with Arc en Ciel+ and Alternative Côte d'Ivoire, two HIV/AIDS-focused NGOs founded by Ivorian men who have sex with men. The involvement of these Ivorian groups in promoting the prevention and treatment of HIV/AIDS sustained them for many years, and continues to be the main aim of their programming, and their main source of funding, today.

As Thomann (2014) has documented, the relationship between Heartland and these Ivorian organizations is, perhaps unsurprisingly, wildly imbalanced. As the party bringing money to the table, Heartland has most, if not all, of the power. While activists from Arc en Ciel+ and Alternative Côte d'Ivoire might be the ones on the front lines, ultimately their work is evaluated using metrics developed by bureaucrats on the other side of the Atlantic. The Ivorians' lives are dependent on making the fruits of their labor—the number of people they get to undergo testing, for example, and the number of people they help get on a treatment plan—intelligible to these outsiders.

This dynamic has produced both winners and losers among sexual minorities in Côte d'Ivoire. Without question, access to foreign funding has enhanced the prestige and capacity of Arc en Ciel+ and Alternative Côte d'Ivoire. But it has done so at the expense of sexual minority activists' ability to push priorities that have little to do with the fight against HIV/AIDS, such as promoting the economic empowerment of lesbians and bisexual women or creating safe spaces for gender non-conforming Ivorians.

More broadly, the ties to Western activists have empowered Ivorians who are comfortable speaking these Westerners' language—in describing the work they do, but also in describing who they are. Over time, Ivorian activists have increasingly embraced terminology that signals fluency in Western LGBT rights activism. Words like *branché*, *yossi* and *woubi* remain in use, but they are increasingly accompanied by words like gay, homo and MSM, for men who have sex with men. (Curiously, the French equivalent, HSH, for *les hommes ayant des relations sexuelles avec des hommes*, has never caught on.)

The spread of this language has real consequences. By using the Westerners' words, members of Arc en Ciel+ and Alternative Côte d'Ivoire broadcast that their organizations represent Ivorians who see themselves much like Westerners do. For men like Brahima, who has always had an ambiguous relationship to this identity-based vocabulary and viewed many of the men who adopt it as needlessly indiscreet, these organizations, intended to be places of refuge, have instead become places to avoid.

* * *

The marginalization of people who aren't gay men, or who don't feel comfortable identifying as such, is perhaps best captured by the fate of Côte d'Ivoire's *travesti* movement. *Travestis*, a word used to refer to people who were designated male at birth but publicly identify or present as women all or part of the time, have been organizing for decades in Abidjan, often more effectively than the country's other sexual minorities (Thomann and Corey-Boulet 2015). In the 1990s, before Côte d'Ivoire's economic and political crises gave way to violence, they were forceful in asserting their rights. They organized meetings and parties, and they pushed back against press coverage they viewed as tasteless or sensational. In 1994, "sarcastic reporting" about one of their meetings by the newspaper *Soir Info* inspired them to attack its offices, "assaulting journalists and breaking a number of windows," Nguyen (2010) writes. This incident led them to form a group: *L'association des travestis de Côte d'Ivoire.*

A 1998 documentary, *Woubi Chéri*, by the directors Philip Brooks and Laurent Bocahut, captures what life was like during this time for Abidjan's *travestis*, many of whom were sex workers. About halfway through the film we see footage of two *travestis*, Bibiche and Tatiana, chasing after clients who drive by on dark, near-empty streets. The *travestis* describe their lives as difficult but manageable. Sex work—or "whoring," as Bibiche calls it—has been profitable. "I thought I'd make a few bucks whoring and that's what I did," she explains. "I have my own furnished place thanks to whoring. I say, thank God for whoring!"

The tone of the film is generally hopeful. What little plot there is centers on the *travestis* organizing a party, and ends with Barbara, the group's leader, getting a kiss on the cheek from a man who raps for her. "I do battle every day when I'm out and about," Barbara says, describing the struggle against stigmatization. "It's like cleaning a house that's constantly dirty. You just have to keep cleaning."

Not long after *Woubi Chéri* came out, however, Barbara moved to France, where she lives today. *L'association des travestis de Côte d'Ivoire* disbanded; many members are believed to be dead. No group has taken its place.

Thomann (2014) argues that the Ivorian *travesti* movement has been a casualty of international efforts to support other sexual minorities, primarily men like the members of Arc en Ciel+ and Alternative Côte d'Ivoire working to combat HIV/AIDS. *Travestis'* "militant activism," he writes, "fizzled and has been completely erased in the context of the nonprofit industrial complex, which focuses on 'men who have sex with men' and channels money into organizations that represent them. *Travestis* have limited involvement with these organizations, often interacting with them only to receive free condoms."

The erasure Thomann describes came into sharp focus following Côte d'Ivoire's post-election conflict in late 2010 and early 2011. The fighting began after Gbagbo contested, and rejected, the results of the 2010 presidential election, which showed he had lost to Alassane Ouattara. Fighters loyal to Ouattara, led by the rebels who had taken over the country's north after the coup attempt in 2002, faced off against Gbagbo's loyalists in months of brutal conflict that culminated in the Battle of Abidjan in late March and early April 2011. Ultimately, French and UN troops intervened on Ouattara's behalf, and Gbagbo was arrested in his residence.

For Côte d'Ivoire's *travesti* population, the formal end of the conflict only brought new threats to their security. For more than a year after Ouattara's inauguration, the fighters who had aided him, and who subsequently installed themselves in Abidjan in peacetime, singled out *travesti* sex workers for all kinds of abuses. Rounding them up from bars and from the streets, these soldiers took *travesti* sex workers back to their bases, beating them, stripping them naked and, sometimes, anally raping them with their Kalashnikov rifles.

Some of the *travestis* blamed this behavior on the fact that many of the pro-Ouattara soldiers were Muslim—a view that reflected religious tensions stirred by the fighting. But a more common, and more plausible, explanation was that they had never been to Abidjan before and were wholly unexposed to the type of environment in which *travesti* sex workers would be permitted to live and work somewhat openly. "They come from the bush up in the north," Claver Touré, the executive director of Alternative Côte d'Ivoire, told me during an interview for a story about the attacks I wrote for the Associated Press. "They can't read. They don't have an open mind. They came to Abidjan just because of the post-election crisis and they saw gay people for the first time in their lives. And they thought, 'Oh, that's what that is. That's what we call homosexuality.'"

Regardless of what was driving the abuses, the inability of the *travestis* to mount any kind of protest underscored the fact that their 1990s-era activism was a thing of the past. When I began my reporting for AP, one of the *travestis* who had been attacked told me that, if I wanted anyone to read it, I should expand its focus to cover abuses against sexual minorities writ large. "No one will care if it's just about *travestis*," she said.

* * *

In recent years, the focus of foreign donors has begun to expand somewhat beyond the fight against HIV/ AIDS. This process was given a push in 2011, when the administration of US President Barack Obama took up the issue.

In December of that year, the White House issued a memorandum empowering "all agencies engaged abroad to ensure that U.S. diplomacy and foreign assistance promote and protect the human rights of LGBT persons" (Presidential Memorandum 2011). According to the memorandum, these agencies were directed to devise steps to combat the criminalization of same-sex sexual acts and ensure that the US government would come up with "swift and meaningful" responses to the human rights abuses of sexual minorities. The release of the memorandum coincided with a widely covered speech by Hillary Clinton, then the secretary of state, at the UN Human Rights Council in Geneva. Echoing a line she had used in reference to women more than fifteen years earlier at a United Nations conference in Beijing, Clinton (2011) declared, "Gay rights are human rights and human rights are gay rights."

In many ways, the memorandum was a way for the Obama administration to catch up to what other European donor countries were already doing. Yet because of the influence the US government has with African officials, combined with the way many African sexual minorities idealize American culture, it registered as a significant event.

On the ground in Abidjan, US Embassy officials began establishing deeper contacts at Arc en Ciel+ and Alternative Côte d'Ivoire, and the ambassador began hosting activists at his residence for a reception to mark LGBTI

Pride Month. Other donors, too, became more visible in their outreach to Ivorian sexual minorities. And instead of exclusively emphasizing the public health aspect of this work, as had often been the case in the past, they were more willing to frame this outreach as part of their general human rights advocacy. In June 2013, the French Embassy allocated roughly €45,000 for programming that would promote the rights of "homosexuals," transgender people and sex workers. Claver Touré credited France's ramped-up engagement in the issue with facilitating a meeting between Alternative Côte d'Ivoire and representatives of the Ivorian justice ministry—the first such meeting his group had ever been granted.

As donors more forcefully expressed interest in promoting sexual minorities' human rights, groups like Alternative Côte d'Ivoire slowly became more inclusive. This shift was motivated at least in part out of fear that, if they didn't, they would lose access to the new funding that was becoming available. Touré began promoting women to leadership positions within the organization and encouraging *travestis* who had primarily used its head-quarters as a safe space to become more actively involved in programming. It's worth noting, too, that he discouraged *travestis* from forming their own organizations, despite the fact that many *travestis* were justifiably skeptical that Alternative, which had for so long been geared toward responding to the needs of gay men, could effectively represent their interests.

At the same time, the ever-growing influence of Western donors reinforced Ivorian activists' embrace of Western terminology. This continued to discourage the active participation of men like Brahima, who did not necessarily see a place for themselves within the well-defined, relatively inflexible LGBT taxonomy.

Moreover, the increased visibility of Alternative Côte d'Ivoire and Arc en Ciel+ exposed their members to the kind of backlash that often greets sexual minorities when they become more emboldened. One night in January 2014, a crowd gathered outside Touré's residence, not far from Alternative Côte d'Ivoire's headquarters. Touré and two other Alternative staffers had just returned from work when they heard whistling and the banging of pots and pans outside. As their numbers swelled to about sixty, the demonstrators started chanting "The house of the *pédés*" and "We don't want *pédés*." They threw garbage, including human excrement, on the grounds of the villa and, as the Alternative staffers huddled inside, tried to break down the gate using stones and iron bars, stopping only when police showed up.

Two days later, a similar gathering took place outside the headquarters itself. This time, the mob posted anti-gay slogans on the exterior of the property: "No to *pédés*," "Stop the homos" and, on the gate, "You were made by your mother and father and you will end up with a woman, not a man." Three days after that, a significantly larger crowd encountered little resistance as it ransacked the building in broad daylight, sending a security guard to the hospital with wounds to his face, causing $12,000 in property damage and looting or destroying more than $35,000 worth of equipment.

Though they failed to pressure Ivorian authorities to step in and prevent the attack, the US Embassy and PEPFAR representatives did help Touré and his colleagues cope with the aftermath, providing office space for them as the headquarters building was rehabilitated. Two years later, however, another high-profile attack on sexual minorities came as a direct result of Embassy staffers' carelessness.

In June 2016, the Embassy organized a condolence book to honor victims of the shooting at Pulse, the gay nightclub in Orlando. Prominent Ivorian officials, including the prime minister at the time, signed the book, as did six members of Arc en Ciel+. Photos of these men signing the book were published on the Embassy's website, accompanied with a caption that identified them as members of the "LGBTI community." Within days, two of the men were assaulted in their neighborhoods, and four of them, including the two who'd been attacked, were forced to leave their homes after facing backlash from friends and relatives.

Such incidents only reinforced Brahima's fear that associating with the country's most prominent organizations working on behalf of sexual minorities would expose him to personal risk. This fear meant that, as the Ivorian movement continued to evolve and make gains, he would remain on the sidelines.

10

Brahima du jardin

When Brahima was a child, his best friend, the only person he saw as a confidante, was his kid sister, Fatoumata. She was a few years younger and proved a dependable ally: They backed each other up in schoolyard fights and helped each other out with cash when they could. In high school, when Brahima needed money to keep up with his new, wealthier friends, Fatoumata—whose formal education had ended by then—would slip him small notes from what she earned selling fish at the market. And she never told anyone that the small sums their parents gave him, intended for books and meals, were going instead toward club covers and whiskey.

Fatoumata lived with the family until she turned eighteen, when a primary school teacher from the town of Agboville, north of Abidjan, asked her to marry him. She went to stay with this man even before the marriage was formalized, but toward the end of 1993 she returned, having fallen ill with what appeared to be malaria. Brahima remembers that she was home in December when Houphouët-Boigny, Côte d'Ivoire's beloved founding president, died in office at the age of eighty-eight. That day, she came to Brahima's bedroom to wake him up and report the news. "What will become of us?" she asked him. "It will be very complicated for us!" Fatoumata did not get to see for herself how right she was. A mere twenty days later, she, too, was dead, having never recovered from her illness.

Brahima has never grieved as hard as he did in the weeks that followed. For five days, his mother could do nothing but try to lift him from his bed. Every time he saw Fatoumata's girlfriends around the neighborhood, he experienced anew the shock of her absence. What hurt him the most, he says today, is that Fatoumata never attained what he often describes as a *vie normale*: She did not get married. She did not have children. She did not spend her adult years nurturing a family. "She wasn't able to taste certain things in life," Brahima says. "She left us very young."

Since returning from Cameroon to Côte d'Ivoire more than a decade ago, Brahima, now in his mid-forties, has been working toward a normal life of his own. But in Côte d'Ivoire there are few good models for the life of a

man who sleeps with men, whether openly or not, and his
recent trajectory has been as peripatetic as ever.

When he arrived at the Ivorian–Ghanaian border in
early 2006, his brother met him and drove him back to his
home in Abidjan's Plateau district. There, Brahima tried his
best to keep to himself, avoiding friends who had expected
him to return bearing gifts and stories of success overseas.

As he went about trying to reestablish himself, he
lost several years pursuing ideas that went nowhere. His
plan to sell uniforms to mechanics ran aground when he
discovered that other companies had locked up most of
the clients. His plan for a marketing company promoting
concerts and parties failed to attract the necessary start-up
funds. As he awaited new inspiration, he started working
part-time at his cousin's cybercafé.

Around this time, he reconnected with a friend of his,
Monique, a hairdresser he had known from his Adjamé
days. They had slept together periodically for two years
or so in the late 1990s, though this ended when Monique
learned that Brahima was seeing Muriel, one of her clients.
Enraged, Monique came over to Brahima's apartment
to confront them one morning, smashing Brahima's
Motorola flip phone when he confirmed that the rumors
were true. They stopped speaking, and Brahima soon left
for Cameroon.

Now, Monique reentered his life a changed woman,
a born-again Christian. Upon hearing Brahima was back
in town, she started calling him and helping him out with

small gifts—a new shirt here, a pair of shoes there—while he struggled to break even financially. Eventually, the two began talking about dating, though Monique insisted this could only happen if Brahima was looking to marry.

"I was coming out of a period where I was far from everyone," Brahima says, explaining why he accepted. "I had a need of being loved. I had a need of people who could trust me, who could share a point of view with me. I didn't hesitate to marry because, as we say all the time, it's stability. It permits you to be stable, to be organized, to have a model life and all that."

They wed in a large, festive ceremony in Abidjan, though signs of trouble emerged soon after. Monique's view of Brahima became colored by her clients, who frowned on the match. "The clients at the salon were *grandes dames*, with husbands who had a lot of means, big cars, lots of money," Brahima says. "Her friends spoke of these extraordinary husbands, and her husband didn't even have a job. He was good for nothing. They put this in her head." She soon grew tired of supporting him and impatient for his circumstances to improve. "She complained all the time," he says. "About everything."

An even bigger problem, though, was the couple's inability to conceive. Monique had no children, and starting a family was clearly her primary motivation for marrying. After several miscarriages, she became convinced that the problem lay with Brahima—even though he had already fathered two children—and demanded he visit her pastor.

Brahima obliged, only to be told by the pastor that he was possessed by a demon.

The marriage folded soon after that. Brahima and Monique stopped speaking. When Brahima left poems and love notes on Monique's pillow in the morning, he'd return from the cybercafé at the end of the day to find them in the trash, ripped to pieces. Then, one day only six or seven months after their wedding, he came home to an empty house. Monique had packed her things and gone to stay at the church. Brahima did not run after her.

Though Monique has twice tried to reconcile, Brahima has refused. Instead he has remained single, having apparently given up, at least for now, on the idea that his *vie normale* will be realized through a stable relationship.

The most important person in his life these days is Fatim, the daughter he fathered when he was twenty-five. She is in her early twenties now, only slightly older than Brahima's younger sister, Fatoumata, was when she died, and he speaks of her in a similar way, as a confidante. She comes to visit him when he's in the city, and they go out for drinks. To Brahima's great amusement, they are sometimes mistaken for a couple. "She is proud of the fact that her father is me, that he is young, he is in style," Brahima says.

Brahima dreams one day of opening up to her about his sexuality. He knows he must tread carefully, however, fearing rejection and even blackmail if she takes the news badly. "For now, I can't confide in her, but I'm going to watch her evolution," he says. "The problem is that she and I have not lived in the same house for a very long time. I don't know her current mentality."

Whatever her prejudices, he believes—and perhaps depends on this belief—that with time he can convince her to accept him. "I know her," he says, matter-of-factly. "That's my girl." This may not lead to the normal life he's always wanted, but at least it would give him, for the first time since Cameroon, a relationship in which he could reveal all of himself—including the parts he's been forced for so long to hide.

* * *

In 2015, after a decade of moving from hustle to hustle in the informal economy, Brahima found the job he thought would finally bring him some semblance of financial security. A new hotel in Abidjan's Yopougon district hired him as a manager, offering a monthly salary of $160—the national minimum wage is around $100—as well as rent-free housing and meals at a nearby restaurant. With that kind of compensation, Brahima thought he would soon be able to afford an apartment of his own, far from the eyes of colleagues and relatives, or perhaps even save enough money to apply for a visa to Europe or the United States.

Like so many of Brahima's plans, however, this turned out to be overly optimistic. The Ministry of Tourism moved slowly in granting the hotel a permit, meaning it couldn't advertise and attract clients. For several months in a row, the hotel's owners asked Brahima to forgo his salary until the hotel could establish itself. Brahima went along with this for a while, but finally, in June, worried about settling into a long-term arrangement that was doomed to fail, he quit.

Brahima had certainly experienced disappointment before, but there was something especially dispiriting about this latest setback. He realized he had spent a decade in Abidjan with little to show for it, and he became seized by the notion that he needed to leave his home country once again.

Inspired by stories of Ivorians doing well for themselves in Mali, he traveled in June by road to Bamako. But he was unable to reach the few people he knew in the city ahead of time, and these contacts also failed to return Brahima's calls once he arrived, leaving Brahima dependent on a taxi driver to find a family to take him in. He concedes that the move, conceived in a state of mild despair, was poorly planned. He stayed two weeks before admitting to himself that "everything was in flux" and returning home, now out of a job and forced to ask friends to front the bus fare.

This failure did not rid Brahima of his wish to get away. "I had left Abidjan with a heart to go somewhere else and succeed," he says. He had also hoped to resume dating men, "to find myself somewhere where I would feel freer in my activities, in my actions." As an alternative, he settled on Yamoussoukro, a town in central Côte d'Ivoire. He again left Abidjan by road, taking with him around $80, a backpack and a duffel bag filled with shoes and clothes.

Three decades earlier, in an essay for *The New Yorker*, V.S. Naipaul (1984) had described Yamoussoukro as a place that "awaited full use." He meant this in the most fundamental way. The previous year, Houphouët-Boigny, known to many by that point simply as Le Vieux, or The Old One, had established the town, his birthplace, as the country's political capital, but the business of government had not yet relocated from Abidjan, the cosmopolitan metropolis down on the coast. This largely remains the case today. The absence of activity renders Yamoussoukro's purpose-built environment, however ambitious and impressive, disorienting. The wide boulevards, golf course and fourteen-story Hôtel Président, capped with its top-floor restaurant sandwiched between two horizontal slabs of concrete, seem to have been designed for a population that never arrived.

The phrase "awaited full use" also applied in another, more abstract sense, speaking to the awkward way in which the town carried its conflicted identity. An old brochure for the hotel, described by Naipaul, hints at its animating tension: "Find the traces of the native village of President Houphouët-Boigny," it reads, "and discover the ultra-modern prefiguration of the Africa of tomorrow." The past and the future, together in the same space: this is not an impossible or even a necessarily difficult vision to execute, yet the general air of Yamoussoukro suggests an autocrat's enthusiasms run wild, and a lack of thought given to the integration of competing elements. Hovering above everything, the most stable point on the horizon, is La Basilique Notre Dame de la Paix, a Catholic basilica larger even than St. Peter's in the Vatican. A marvel of soaring columns and stained glass whose dome reaches 158 meters into the air, the basilica is Houphouët-Boigny's most staggering vanity project but also his most curious, given that it was completed—at an estimated cost of $300 million, a figure often said to have doubled the country's national debt—as Côte d'Ivoire's boom was going bust.

Over time, following Houphouët-Boigny's death in 1993 and the onset of political conflict, Yamoussoukro settled into its role as a second-tier tourist destination, overshadowed by the beaches of Grand-Bassam and Assinie. A visitor's day could begin with a morning tee time, followed by a tour of the basilica and a late afternoon at the hotel pool.

This was certainly not what Le Vieux had envisioned. But if the town's residents, to say nothing of the tourists, were happy with the arrangement, couldn't the project be considered a success?

* * *

Arriving in Yamoussoukro, Brahima chose to focus on the town's potential. His new home could be whatever he wanted, or needed, it to be. As in Mali, his few contacts in Yamoussoukro weren't around to welcome him when he got there. He was also turned away from a mosque and a church, so he spent his first nights sleeping in an abandoned bus station. But to those who declined to help him, he responded with bravado. "I said to them, 'You will see me succeed in Yamoussoukro. I'm not leaving.'"

Eager to learn a new field, he convinced a bakery owner to take him on as an apprentice. The arrangement allowed him to eat and sleep at the bakery and bathe in a nearby public bathroom, but after one month he grew discouraged with the menial labor—cleaning, crushing ice—he'd been assigned. "After a while, I said, 'What is happening? I didn't come here to do that.' I said to them that if I couldn't do other things, I'd leave."

Aimless again, he began roaming the streets in search of work, spending nights with the few friends he'd made. "During this time, because no one knew me, people were afraid," he says. "They thought I was a police officer working on an investigation, because I was very well dressed. Others said, 'You need to be wary of him. Is he not a rebel? Is he not a jihadist?' They attributed to me whatever they could attribute to me. But today, I walk by them with pride."

Brahima's luck changed when, out drinking one night, he met a woman named Mariam, the fifty-year-old daughter of a soldier in the presidential guard who had spent her entire life in Yamoussoukro. She was sitting by herself, reading a pamphlet distributed by Jehovah's Witnesses. Brahima, always easy with strangers, struck up a conversation. He learned that Mariam's two children lived in France, and that her siblings were in London and

Abidjan, leaving her alone in the family compound. They talked about God and religion—Mariam is an evangelical Christian, while Brahima comes from a Muslim family but converted to Christianity—and before long she invited him back for a plate of kabato, a northern dish of cornmeal paste. She offered him a spare bedroom in her home, the largest in a courtyard in Yamoussoukro's mostly Muslim neighborhood of Dioulabougou. Meeting Mariam was the luckiest thing that had happened to Brahima in some time. "We found each other in the difficulty of life," he says.

His housing secure, Brahima renewed his search for work. One day, he dropped in on the Café Royal, a restaurant and nightclub on a boulevard running along a lake. After talking his way into the manager's office, he recounted the story of his failure in Mali and described his reluctance to return to Abidjan, his desire to establish himself in this new place. The manager turned out to be the older brother of some of Brahima's friends from the high school he attended in Abidjan before flunking out. The man took a liking to Brahima and gave him his card. From that point on, Brahima called the manager every Monday morning, determined not to be forgotten.

One day in early August, the manager told Brahima to come by the café that afternoon. "I understood right away that he had good news for me," Brahima says. At the meeting, the manager explained that, beginning on August 7, the anniversary of Côte d'Ivoire's independence, he wanted Brahima to set up tables in the outdoor garden across the street from the café. If diners took to the space, Brahima could manage it on a regular basis, earning $65 a month in salary along with whatever he could make in tips.

Brahima tackled this new project with the hunger of an intern—which, despite being forty-four years old, despite having worked for more than two decades, he effectively was. He befriended local sex workers and told them to use the garden, knowing their presence would attract men with money to spend on chicken and beer. He promoted the space on 88.1 FM Radio JAM, the local station with the largest reach. And he made a point of charming his wealthy clients, encouraging them to return again and again. The job played to the strengths of a natural networker, a man who since childhood had been able to identify the most important people in a room or at a party and win them over by dint of his ear for anecdote, his ability to fill long gaps of unstructured time with fawning introductions, pleasantries and debate.

Within months, the space was thriving, rivaling the Café Royal itself. From Thursday night through Sunday night, the plastic tables scattered across the grass were occupied until well after midnight. Though Brahima's salary was somewhat irregular, he supported himself with tips, aided by the fact that he lived rent-free with Mariam. Meanwhile, he assumed an identity inextricably linked to his success: *Brahima du jardin*, or Brahima of the garden, the moniker that staff and customers typically used when addressing him.

With this new name came a new look: that of an Ivorian dandy. Though Brahima always took pride in his appearance, in Abidjan he rarely deviated from polo shirts and button-downs paired with dark jeans. In Yamoussoukro, by contrast, he amassed a collection of golf caps in an array of colors. Dark sunglasses covered his eyes at all hours. If the night was cool, he would sometimes don a blazer and bowtie. He explains that these flourishes were a necessary aspect of his new job. "People look at your appearance before they form an opinion of you," he says. "That's part of life. Who wouldn't want to look at something that is beautiful?"

It was clear, too, that Brahima was using his look to struggle against boundaries that had restricted him for years, preventing him from embracing his sexuality. Shortly before leaving for Yamoussoukro, Brahima had declared that he was "tired of pretending" to be a straight man, and he held out hope that the town could be the place where pretending finally became unnecessary. In his right ear he began wearing a gaudy blue fake diamond as well as a teal band featuring the interlocking Cs of the Chanel logo. The earrings are "only a style that I like," Brahima said, though he also knew they were loaded visual cues. Seeing them, some Ivorians would conclude he is gay, while others would assume he's "a gangster," "a bandit," someone "outside the law." Brahima welcomed all of these interpretations. His lack of concern reflected the freedom he felt in Yamoussoukro, something he hadn't experienced since his days in Yaoundé, when he dated Thierry.

Yet Brahima retained the caution of a man still uncertain of just how much of himself to put forward, a man awaiting full use. Asked whether he intended to declare his sexuality in a more overt way in Yamoussoukro, he responded that this was not an immediate priority. This move would need to be made in its own time. "It's a bit too early to launch certain actions in my life," he says. "Because when you make yourself discovered you need to make sure you are independent, and that it's not going to rock other aspects of your life."

* * *

One Saturday afternoon a few months after he arrived in Yamoussoukro, Brahima crowded into the booth of Radio JAM with nine other guests for a one-hour talk show. In his short time in town, Brahima had become something of a fixture at the station, appearing frequently on programs hosted by Charley, a DJ who had worked there for nearly fifteen years. Founded in 1997, Radio JAM stands for *Jeunes africains modernes*, or Young modern Africans. It occupies a two-story, faded white building situated halfway between Brahima's garden and the presidential palace.

This particular program dealt with the problem of teenage pregnancy and obstacles to providing sex education to Ivorian youth. The group that joined Brahima and Charley in the booth included two local education officials and three high school students, two girls and a boy. To begin with, they listened to a short sketch about a sixteen-year-old girl, Carole, whose father goes into a rage when he overhears her working on a homework assignment about contraceptive methods. The sketch challenges the teachings of local religious leaders concerning birth control, as well as the easy authority assumed by many Ivorian fathers. "A child is a gift from God, and is never too much," Carole's father lectures. "A mouth that God has produced will always have something with which to be fed." Carole responds dismissively: "The teachers told us that God has nothing to do with it. They said each person is responsible for the children they're going to produce."

After the sketch ended, Charley had the guests introduce themselves before launching into the debate. (*"Brahima du jardin, pour votre plaisir,"* Brahima, speaking slowly and in a low voice, said when his turn came.) Though the discussion that followed was generally supportive of Carole, the hour was not without its moments of tension. At one point, a young woman named Djima, who works at Radio JAM, confronted the education officials, noting they were quick to criticize parents resistant to sex education in schools but did nothing to discipline teachers caught sleeping with—and impregnating—students. An awkward pause followed Djima's comment. One of the officials then tried to downplay the scope of the phenomenon she'd described.

Though Brahima had no real expertise on the subject, he consistently contributed some of the most thoughtful comments, drawing on his experiences as a parent while evincing his own hard-won faith in the importance of individual responsibility and self-reliance. No one party can be blamed for teenage pregnancy, he said, but students ultimately need to take charge of their own lives. "The true problem is that students need to be made to understand that it's their lives, their future," he said. "Who is going to carry the burden? It's the students."

The program showcased Ivorians' general openness to discussing subjects that were once considered inappropriate and risqué. Brahima told the audience it would have been difficult for him, as a child, to bring up contraception with his parents. "In Africa, all subjects related to sexuality are taboo," he said. "When I was young, in a religious family, there were certain debates that I just couldn't have with my elders." Yet despite the shift demonstrated by the show, afterward, away from the other guests, Brahima said he believed there was still an impenetrable barrier to any public discussion of alternative sexuality that wasn't explicitly, and enthusiastically, censorious. He said he wouldn't dream of raising the issue with anyone in the booth, even those—like Charley and Djima—who seemed more interested in facilitating debate than pushing their own views.

Brahima's fears had been reinforced the previous month by a mini-scandal in Côte d'Ivoire's music industry. In early November, *La Tribune Ivoirienne*, a newspaper, had reported that the son of the late Roger Fulgence Kassy, a television personality credited with launching the careers of a number of famous Ivorian performers, had married another man in the United States. The article quoted an aunt of Thierry Kassy, the son, who said: "If he really married a man, that means he's no longer my nephew because when we say nephew, we are talking about a man. He needs to marry a woman because he's a man. He needs to marry a woman to procreate, to make children to pass down the name of his father." An uncle said: "It's beyond me, really, I can't believe my eyes. It's very bizarre for me. Like I'm dreaming and need to return to earth."

In Yamoussoukro, Brahima says, reaction to reports of the marriage had been much the same. "Africa is very complicated," he says. "People say, 'How can the son of a big man like that become a homo?'" Instead of humanizing sexual minorities, the fact that a member of a well-regarded family was openly gay only underscored, for many Ivorians, how homosexuality could touch anyone who wasn't careful.

These kinds of scandals are not unusual in Cote d'Ivoire. In the music industry, especially, rumors of homosexuality seem to swirl around anyone who makes it big, at least for a time. For sexual minority activists, the scandals represent opportunity as much as danger. The activists are generally open anyway, and press coverage of alternative sexualities, whether real or merely suspected, allows for conversations that can be difficult to broach otherwise. If they're especially skilled, they can steer these discussions in a productive direction, moving away from strict condemnation and toward understanding of the lives sexual minorities lead and the challenges they face.

But for Brahima, who steers clear of activists and activism in general, these scandals reaffirm his commitment to staying in the shadows. He remains committed to his approach of pursuing material success first, personal and romantic fulfillment later. Most openly gay and bisexual men he reads about are celebrities. Haven't their achievements contributed to their freedom, their ability to live their lives as they want? "Take for example Elton John," Brahima says over a beer during a slow afternoon in his garden. "Do you think he has problems with his sexuality? A great musician like that? Who will bother him?" Brahima doesn't think he needs to attain Elton John levels of fame and fortune. But what he does need before going public with his alternative sexuality, he says, is sufficient financial security to protect himself from social sanction and from claims that he's not a true Ivorian—the same claims that Thierry Kassy, happily married and living in the United States, can presumably tune out.

The problem for Brahima, though, is that he's Ivorian through and through, and as such he faces the same obstacles to financial success that have bedeviled all men of his generation—men who were born too late to benefit from the Ivorian miracle engineered by Houphouët-Boigny in the 1960s, 1970s and 1980s, and who instead endured more than two decades of political turmoil. Having seen for himself the tail end of the country's economic boom as a boy, and having eagerly consumed all the information he's ever encountered, true and false, about life in more prosperous parts of the world, he has an acute sense of the extent to which his country has let him down. "Without being too prideful," he says, "do you really think, if I were in the US, with the intelligence that I have, I couldn't get a better job?"

His experiences in Yamoussoukro have nonetheless made him the most optimistic he's been in years. Only time will tell whether he's actually getting somewhere or merely running in place, but he has chosen to believe that the former is the case. "It's today that I am afraid of dying. When I was in Abidjan, I wasn't afraid of that," he says. "It's when you are fulfilled that you have this fear."

PART 3
LIBERIA

11

Everybody will carry their own burden

In January 2012, the Liberian newspaper *New Dawn* published a story that featured a startling claim. Western lobbyists, the paper reported, had promised to give $4 million to members of the Liberian Senate and House of Representatives who would be willing to support legislation "guaranteeing the rights of gays and lesbians." The influence effort was purportedly being led by the "Foundation for the Protection of Gay Rights," an organization that *New Dawn* said was based in California.

The story, written by the journalist E.J. Nathaniel Daygbor (2012), was entirely of a piece with a national media sector that tends toward the sensational. Sitting at the crossroads of two favored topics—sex and political malfeasance—it attracted considerable attention, and versions of it soon appeared in other papers. This is despite the fact that even the most cursory fact-checking would have revealed a fundamental flaw: There was no evidence that the "Foundation for the Protection of Gay Rights" actually existed. The organization had no online footprint, and the various media outlets' sources had offered no evidence of the alleged proposal.

Shortly after his story ran, I met with Daygbor at a café in central Monrovia. It was late on a weekday afternoon, and the place was nearly dead, but he nevertheless chose a table in the back corner and spoke to me in hushed tones. He told me that he had received his information from three lawmakers who granted interviews on condition of anonymity. In the moment, this had seemed strong enough to run with. But now that the story was out in the world, he conceded, with a smile and a shrug, that he had probably been duped.

In Liberia, as elsewhere, newspapers that prove to be poor sources of verifiable facts can all the same offer a window into national anxieties. In this case, Daygbor's story and those that followed coincided with a sharp uptick in concern about Western LGBT rights campaigners, who were suspected of deploying considerable financial resources to promote an agenda that Liberians—and other Africans, the thinking went—would never endorse on their own.

Other media coverage from this period reflects just how widespread this concern had become. "The so-called developed world is doing everything within their power to coerce the rest of the world to allow homosexuality to be practiced, referring to it as 'gay rights,'" read a fairly typical editorial published by the *National Chronicle*, another newspaper. In its own editorial, *New Dawn* accused the United States of conditioning foreign aid on legal protections for sexual minorities, describing the practice as a "new form of subjugation that Africa should resist with unison." Other newspapers ran front-page stories about the "spread" of homosexuality within Liberia, pairing them with photos ripped from the internet of unidentified black men kissing (Corey-Boulet 2014).

For months, only one newspaper, *FrontPage Africa*, went to the trouble of interviewing actual sexual minorities in Liberia. The rest seemed content to publish reports of homosexual "recruitment" sourced back to religious leaders and other homophobic public figures. The apparent goal of this reporting was to marshal public opinion against a perceived threat to Liberian culture and values. At one point, *Women Voices*, which billed itself as "Liberia's Most Equitable Newspaper," published an editorial titled "Gays & Lesbians Must Not Be Given Any Rights."

Such opinions were not new in Liberia. They surfaced whenever the topic of alternative sexualities came up. But prior to late 2011, the topic hardly ever came up. And when it did, it was only rarely framed as something that had any domestic relevance.

* * *

What had changed, then? Why was an issue that had previously been treated largely as a curiosity suddenly sparking fevered debates about sovereignty and national identity?

The answer, in the eyes of LGBT activists and political analysts, was the Obama administration's memorandum, issued in December 2011, empowering US government agencies to place more emphasis on LGBT issues in their work overseas. The memorandum called for allocating foreign assistance to promote LGBT rights. But many Liberians, and many Africans, assumed its real mission was to cut foreign assistance to countries where those rights were violated.

The memorandum—coupled with Hillary Clinton's speech at the Human Rights Council in which she declared that "gay rights are human rights, and human rights are gay rights"—was by no means the first time a Western government had weighed in on the issue. Just two months earlier, David Cameron, then Britain's prime minister, had given an interview to the BBC in which he indicated that other countries' LGBT rights records would influence London's decisions about foreign aid.

"We are not just talking about it. We are also saying that British aid should have more strings attached," Cameron said in the interview, which was recorded during the 2011 Commonwealth summit in Perth, Australia. "This is an issue where we are pushing for movement, we are prepared to put some money behind what we believe ... Britain is one of the premier aid givers in the world. We want to see countries that receive our aid adhering to proper human rights" (BBC 2011).

In soliciting reaction from African public figures to the interventions from Washington and London, Western journalists, perhaps inadvertently, illustrated a common problem with how debates about LGBT rights in Africa have been covered in recent years. The Africans interviewed for these stories were not being invited to discuss the issue on their own terms, but instead to respond to what Westerners were doing and saying. What the journalists were after, fundamentally, were signs of dissent and, even better, outright conflict. Certain hardline religious leaders, as well as politicians like Zimbabwe's Mugabe, were more than happy to oblige, seizing the opportunity to once again demonstrate their homophobic bona fides. Their quotes tended to get the most publicity.

But other Africans who were asked to comment suggested that they were genuinely grappling with the implications of the American and British policies, along with larger questions about their countries' openness to social change. These quotes were messier, and more difficult to slot into 800-word news stories that weren't even necessarily about Africa. Unsurprisingly, they tended to get less attention.

In Uganda, for example, debates about homosexuality had been raging well before Obama, Clinton and Cameron spoke up. Two years before the December 2011 memorandum, the country had become practically synonymous with homophobia when a lawmaker introduced a bill calling for those convicted of "aggravated homosexuality" to be executed. Though the bill had stalled by 2011, it signaled an increasingly hostile climate for LGBT rights activists. In January 2011, David Kato, an activist whose face had appeared on the front page of a local newspaper calling for sexual minorities to be killed—"Hang Them," the headline read—was bludgeoned to death in his home with a hammer.

Uganda, then, was a natural starting point for journalists seeking a (reactionary) foil to the (progressive) policies adopted by the US and the UK. At first glance, John Nagenda, a senior adviser to President Yoweri Museveni, seemed to fit the bill nicely. "I don't like her tone, at all," he said, referring to Clinton's speech. "Homosexuality here is taboo, it's something anathema to Africans, and I can say that this idea of Clinton's, of Obama's, is something that will be seen as abhorrent in every country on the continent that I can think of" (Pflanz 2011).

But that was only part of his statement. The second half, which was less widely quoted, left open the possibility for change, however slow. "A very, very slowly increasing number of Ugandans, and I am one of them, see homosexuals as full human beings who can do what they like in private, between consenting adults," he said. "But people look at me like I am a very funny fish when I say these things, even in my own household, such is the way that these things are looked at on this continent."

A similar dynamic was on display two years later, when Obama traveled to Africa and, in an indirect way, was made to answer for the policy in person for the first time. His visit, which began in Dakar, Senegal, coincided with the Supreme Court ruling in *United States* v. *Windsor*, which struck down the Defense of Marriage Act. During a joint press conference with Senegalese President Macky Sall, a member of the traveling press corps asked Obama for his reaction to the ruling and also asked Sall whether he would "work to decriminalize homosexuality in this country" ("Remarks" 2013).

Like Nagenda, Sall offered a relatively nuanced take on the issue. True, he did note early in his response that the US and Senegal have "different cultures" and "different traditions." Both the Senegalese and international press, eager as ever to put their finger on a feud, homed in on these words, depicting the exchange as evidence of, as the Associated Press described it, "a clash of cultures."

But Sall said more than that. Like Nagenda in Uganda, he suggested that public opinion on alternative sexualities in Senegal was changing. "Senegal, as far as it is concerned, is a very tolerant country which does not discriminate in terms of inalienable rights of the human being," he said. "We don't tell anybody that he will not be recruited because he is gay or he will not access a job because his sexual orientation is different. But we are still not ready to decriminalize homosexuality."

Similarly layered reactions could be found in Liberia. Yet in the months immediately following the unveiling of the Obama administration memorandum, they were almost entirely drowned out by the more blatantly homophobic ones. The unique positioning of the US in Liberia's national consciousness ensured that the Obama administration's policy would be followed more closely there than perhaps anywhere else, and that the outcry would be especially acute.

* * *

Liberia was founded in the mid-nineteenth century by African-Americans whose travel to West Africa had been bankrolled by the American Colonization Society, or ACS. For various reasons, many of them racist, ACS members had determined that the existence of a free black population in the United States was untenable.

These settlers established an American-style colony and society on the West African coast, setting themselves apart from the indigenous population. In 1847, Liberia declared itself an independent state. Its capital, Monrovia, is named after former US President James Monroe, who was in office when the first ACS-funded ships set sail from New York across the Atlantic Ocean.

While the story of Liberia's origins is fairly well known, it offers only a hint of the full extent of American influence in the country, which remains apparent today in everything from investment flows to street fashion. Local coverage of American politics can be as obsessive as Politico's. Restaurants and shops specialize in American dishes and imported

American goods. At wedding receptions and other parties, the DJs mix hits from New York and Atlanta with those from Abidjan and Lagos. Walking down a street in central Monrovia, it is possible to imagine, if only for a moment, that you've been transported to a louder, stickier version of Brooklyn.

This cultural affinity is matched by the efforts of successive Liberian governments to cultivate close political ties with Washington, a diplomatic strategy that's been central for presidents up through and including the current one, George Weah. No amount of bad behavior on the part of the US, from propping up the corrupt regime of Samuel Doe in the 1980s to exerting the bare minimum of resources toward ending a devastating period of civil conflict that stretched from 1989 to 2003, has dimmed enthusiasm for American friendship and support.

In light of this history, perhaps the most remarkable thing about the backlash to Obama's policy on LGBT rights was the extent to which it reflected a desire on the part of Liberia's political class to create some distance between Monrovia and Washington. Though a major reason for this is the faulty reporting on what the policy actually entailed, journalists weren't the only ones stirring up public anger over the issue of LGBT rights and American support of them.

In early 2012, just as the debate was heating up, a notorious rabble-rouser named Leroy Archie Ponpon co-founded a group named the Movement for Defense of

Gays and Lesbians in Liberia, or MODEGAL, which raised the stakes even higher by orchestrating a public campaign for same-sex marriage in Liberia.

Ponpon's motives were unclear. At the height of his campaign, he agreed to meet with me in the offices of the *Daily Observer*, the newspaper where I was posted as a media trainer for the Canadian NGO Journalists for Human Rights. During our interview, it was obvious that Ponpon relished the attention he was receiving; he grinned as he sparred with the Liberian journalists who popped in to challenge the merits of his cause and tactics. Yet Ponpon did not publicly identify as gay, nor did he coordinate his efforts with anyone who did. When asked directly, he struggled to explain why he had taken up the issue before finally settling on a metaphor that would make many sexual minorities cringe: "Even criminals are entitled to a defense attorney."

Prior to founding MODEGAL, Ponpon had been best known for burning a Norwegian flag to protest the awarding of the Nobel Peace Prize to President Ellen Johnson Sirleaf in 2011. (The prize, issued just days before that year's presidential election, was controversial both for its timing and because of Sirleaf's early support for Charles Taylor, the warlord-turned-president who had been put on trial for war crimes and crimes against humanity.) There was some speculation that Ponpon was working with the political opposition to force Sirleaf, who went on to win the 2011 election, to speak out on the issue of LGBT rights. The issue was politically delicate, as it had the potential to force Sirleaf to alienate either Western donors seeking an expansion of LGBT rights or Liberian voters who resisted such reforms. There was also concern among the diplomatic corps that Ponpon wanted to seek asylum abroad, and that he was using LGBT rights activism to strengthen his case.

Whatever his goal, Ponpon's actions helped fuel the backlash against Liberian sexual minorities. When he appeared in public to make his pitch for same-sex marriage, crowds descended upon him, on one occasion throwing stones at him. The police had to intervene to rescue him at least once. Ponpon also told media outlets that unidentified vigilantes had burned down his mother's house.

Because Ponpon had assumed such a visible role in the debate over LGBT rights, these incidents garnered considerable attention. Yet he was just one of the many people who had their safety compromised during the weeks and months after the Obama administration's memorandum became the biggest story in the country.

During this same period, a group known as the Movement Against Gays in Liberia, or MOGAL, distributed fliers threatening violence against people it identified as supporters of LGBT rights. "Having conducted a comprehensive investigation, we are convinced that the below listed individuals are gays or supporters of the club who don't mean well for our country," the fliers read. "Therefore, we have agreed to go after them using all means in life."

With the potential for mob violence growing, one twenty-six-year-old gay man told me that he and his friends felt they had no choice but to reduce their visibility, at least for a time. "At first, people were so free with everything, but now people are holding back on their dress code," this man said. "Say there's five people, and everybody wants to go out. Someone will decide that we can't go together, because there's a huge possibility that one of us among the group is well known to be a gay. Everybody will carry their own burden. Because some people walk in a feminine way, some people dress in a feminine way. So we say, 'Oh, we can't go together, we'll spread out.'"

This same man said he held out hope that the debate would ultimately create space for Liberians to be more accepting of sexual minorities. In the short term, though, he was focused on his own survival. "It's a good thing for the issue to be in the air, for people to hear about it and get used to hearing about it," he said. "But I feel like for us actually to face it, I don't want to be a part of it. You never know to what extent the people will go."

* * *

The backlash against sexual minorities in Liberia extended from the streets into the corridors of power. Liberian lawmakers, in particular, began pursuing efforts to make the legal climate for sexual minorities more repressive. Under Liberian law, "voluntary sodomy" was already a misdemeanor fetching prison sentences of up to one year, but several officials decided this was insufficient. In the House of Representatives, Clarence Massaquoi introduced a bill to classify "same-sex sexual practices" as a second-degree felony punishable by up to five years in prison. "Homosexuality is not part of our existence as a people," Massaquoi said by way of explaining his bill. "We have never been like that." In the Senate, Jewel Howard Taylor, the ex-wife of Charles Taylor who would go on to become George Weah's running mate in 2017, making her vice president after he won, pushed to make same-sex marriage a first-degree felony punishable by up to ten years behind bars.

Neither of these bills ultimately became law, but they did keep the national conversation focused on sexual minorities, and created more space for homophobic voices to denounce them. Amid this mounting hostility, sexual minorities' ostensible political allies declined to come to their defense.

This included the State Department, whose public statements on LGBT rights had helped to render sexual minorities increasingly vulnerable in the first place. Clinton did not address the issue when she traveled to Liberia in January 2012 for the inauguration ceremony marking the beginning of Sirleaf's second term. The US Embassy in Monrovia also stayed quiet, though diplomats did take time to privately scold journalists, myself included, who questioned whether they were abandoning the very people they claimed to want to help.

Linda Thomas-Greenfield, the US ambassador in Monrovia, who later became assistant secretary of state for African affairs, said this approach partly reflected concerns that further statements from Washington would aggravate the situation rather than calm it. "I think our policy has been extremely clear from Washington that there is not a connection between our long-term aid and policies related to this issue. But knowing how occasionally irresponsible the press is here, my view was that we should not feed that frenzy," she said. "We have given them the information, the correct information. I can't be guaranteed that a public statement that we give will be put out in the way that we want the statement put out."

The isolation of LGBT Liberians was thrown into sharp relief in March 2012, when Sirleaf appeared to defend Liberia's anti-sodomy law in an interview with *The Guardian*. The president became visibly uncomfortable when her questioner, Tamasin Ford, turned to the criminalization of same-sex sexual acts. Asked about the possibility of reforming Liberia's laws, the president said, "I won't sign any law that has to do with that area. None whatsoever." She added, "We've got certain traditional values in our society that we'd like to preserve" (Ford and Allen 2012).

These comments came as a shock to much of the world, especially given that Sirleaf had, just three months earlier, been in Oslo accepting her Nobel. But perhaps even more jarring was the performance of the other participant in the interview: former British Prime Minister Tony Blair, who was in town to promote the work of his charity, the Africa Governance Initiative.

When Ford turned to Blair, who has been hailed in some quarters as a champion of gay rights back home, to ask if he had any "advice" for Sirleaf on how to address the issue of LGBT rights, he simply refused to answer the question, suggesting, with a patronizing smile, that he was too savvy to be drawn into the debate. "One of the advantages of doing what I do now is that I can choose the issues I get into and the issues I don't," he said. "For us the priorities are on power, roads, jobs delivery. I'm not saying these issues aren't important. The president's given her position, and this is not one for me" (Ford and Allen 2012).

It was an awkward, spineless performance on Blair's part. But while it fetched him a fair amount of criticism from British LGBT rights activists, Liberian sexual minorities did not seem especially upset. After all, long before Western politicians started getting involved, they had been making their way without any outside help whatsoever.

12

Anti-Liberian, anti-God

When he was still a teenager—no more than fourteen years old, he thinks—Patrick went to a party one night in the Old Road section of Monrovia. Though the friend who brought him was "somebody I trusted," he didn't know the other people there. Many of the guests, he quickly discovered, were men who slept with other men.

It was the mid-1980s, a time when the city's community of sexual minorities was even more insular than it is today. Young as he was, Patrick had devoted little energy to grappling with his own attraction to men. Before he walked into the house in Old Road, he had no idea a gay scene in Monrovia even existed.

The party did not go well. As guests drank and danced, Patrick found himself in conversation with a man who came onto him—"some influential person who tried to touch me inappropriately," he recalls. At home, Patrick's relatives spoke of sexual minorities with disdain, and he had had limited exposure to Liberians who thought differently. He responded to the advance with aggression. "Because my mom had built in me my self-esteem, I pushed that person off," he says. He was thrown out of the house.

Walking out the front gate, Patrick planned to head back to his home in Mamba Point. Before he could get too far, however, the security guard who had been hired to work the party, and who was stationed outside, called out to him. Patrick explained what had happened, and why he was so upset. The guard seemed to know immediately who Patrick was describing. "Don't mind him," he said. "That's how he behaves."

The guard then offered Patrick a ride home. But that's not, in the end, where they went. Instead, the guard took him to another party, in the neighborhood of Airfield, near Spriggs Payne Airport. The party was a cookout, with a group of men, many of whom identified as gay, eating, drinking and dancing outside in the thick, wet Monrovia air. This time, no one tried to corner Patrick, or to force himself upon him. Patrick decided to stay.

The night gave Patrick his introduction to a world that, while unknown to him, was neither entirely hidden nor entirely open. It was still several years before Charles Taylor would cross into Liberia from neighboring Côte d'Ivoire with about 100 fighters, kicking off the conflicts that would, over the course of nearly a decade and a half, shred the country's social fabric. Though Liberia had experienced a coup in 1980, the country was still at peace, and its gay scene generally adhered to the rhythms of earlier, more prosperous decades.

The precise origins of that scene, the layers of which would reveal themselves to Patrick over several years, are difficult to pin down. But there is a sense among older Liberians that it had existed for a long time, especially among Monrovia's elites. It attracted those who, because of certain, sometimes ineffable qualities—a style of dress, or a way of walking—stood out from the rest of the population. In a 2013 report by Human Rights Watch that described the "passive tolerance" that once prevailed in Liberia, Rev. Dr. Samuel B. Reeves of Monrovia's Providence Baptist Church explained that these people were well-known and faced only limited harassment. Some of them, he said, "even held important positions in both government and the church and were respected in society."

Certainly the scene was well-established by the 1970s, a period that is now remembered fondly for the freedoms it offered, especially when contrasted with the horrors that followed. Nina Simone, who lived in Liberia for three years, would later sing, "You brought me home to Liberia, and all other places are inferior," and the photos from this decade, the glamour they capture, make it easy enough to understand what she meant. Provided they had access to the right circles, and provided they kept quiet about many aspects of their lives when in mixed company, sexual minorities were able to profit from the climate that Simone and others described. When they wanted, they could also peel off and construct spaces tailored specifically for them.

By the time Patrick was coming of age, the network of private homes and other locations where sexual minorities could gather was rich and ever-changing, its boundaries constantly being tested. Wealthy gay and bisexual Liberian men would travel abroad and return wearing "feminine clothing." Sometimes this resulted in "outings" or "incidents," Patrick says, but just as often these men were shielded by their class, and by the fact that the Liberian government included many powerful people who were part of the scene. Foreigners, notably Americans, also contributed to the growing opportunities for sexual minorities to express themselves. Patrick recalls, for example, attending parties hosted by Peace Corps volunteers, who offered up their homes as safe spaces.

Those who lived through this period were not starry-eyed about the possibility that their country would fully embrace them. Hostility was always with them, even when they were ostensibly by themselves, closed off from the public at large. Patrick remembers a number of people who would attend parties organized for sexual minorities and then, while out in the wider world, espouse toxic anti-gay rhetoric. The presence of such people—who identified privately as gay or bisexual while publicly declaring themselves not just straight, but aggressively so—exacerbated the risk of exposure, which was high enough as it was.

Yet despite these challenges, there is an undeniable level of nostalgia among people of Patrick's generation for the prewar years. Whether because of outright acceptance, benign tolerance or plain ignorance, sexual minorities possessed of a certain amount of privilege and savvy could build lives for themselves, however complex. It was a feat that became exponentially more difficult after Taylor invaded and the country collapsed.

* * *

After launching his offensive on Christmas Eve 1989, Taylor addressed the Liberian people via an interview with the BBC, introducing them to his rebel group, the National Patriotic Front of Liberia, or NPFL. He announced his goal of ousting President Samuel Doe, who had led the coup in 1980, though he disavowed any political ambition for himself.

As Stephen Ellis documents in *The Mask of Anarchy* (2001), his landmark book about the Liberian conflicts, the NPFL suffered from internal disorganization and dissension from the outset. But it benefited from the fact that the government it was trying to topple had been badly weakened by Doe's corrupt, inept rule. As the first indigenous Liberian to serve as president, Doe had vowed to refashion the country so that everyone, not just the Americo-Liberian elite, could prosper. However, these promises were undermined by his open hostility to, and his apparent endorsement of violence against, perceived rivals of his own Krahn ethnic group, notably the Gio and Mano.

Taylor's forces had entered Liberia in the north, where there are large concentrations of Gio and Mano people, many of whom, Taylor said, were eager to sign up and fight. "As the NPFL came in, we didn't even have to act," Taylor later claimed (Berkeley 1992). "People came to us and said: 'Give me a gun. How can I kill the man who killed my mother?'" The Liberian army struggled to stop the advance, and within months the rebels were threatening Monrovia.

But divisions within the NPFL were hardening. Before long, Prince Johnson, the commander of an elite group of NPFL fighters, had broken off to lead his own movement, the Independent National Patriotic Front of Liberia, or INPFL. Within months, then, the country had been divided in three, with territory controlled by fighters loyal to Doe, Taylor and Johnson.

One of the Liberians who found himself in INPFL-controlled territory was Tecumsay Roberts, a pop singer whose hits would be familiar to anyone who so much as set foot in a nightclub in Monrovia in the 1980s. The writer Stephanie Horton (2012) has described Roberts as "Liberia's own Michael Jackson," and photographs suggest Roberts encouraged the comparison. The cover photo for his single "Comin' Home" is a mirror image of

Jackson's iconic "Thriller" album cover: It shows Roberts, in a white blazer, lying diagonally across the frame, staring into the camera, his face less severe than Jackson's but similarly captivating.

Throughout Roberts' career, he was trailed by whisperings that he was gay, or in any case that he slept with men. But people knew him primarily for his music—the horns, drums and, above all, the singing that, taken together, showcase West African pop at its catchiest. "Comin' Home" made his attachment to the region, and the continent, explicit. "I've been around the world, from Zanzibar to California," Roberts sings, "but Africa, Africa will always be my home."

In the context of the Liberian wars, though, Roberts' accomplishments, and his fundamental identity as an African, were stripped away. Instead, men under Prince Johnson's command seized on rumors concerning Roberts' sexuality to cast him as something dangerous and foreign, and then made him suffer for it.

INFPL rebels arrested Roberts one night in 1990. In an interview in December 2018 with *FrontPage Africa*, his brother, Sandy Roberts, said the pair had gone out looking for food when they were stopped by Johnson's convoy. After complimenting Tecumsay on his music, Johnson told him to get in the car and go with the convoy to a rebel base to sing for his fighters.

"I was frightened on that day when Johnson was waving his silver pistol in the air and ordering my brother to get into the vehicle. My brother almost wet his pants out of fear," Sandy Roberts, who refers to his brother by the nickname "TR," said. "TR told me he had to go along to get some food for the family and it would have been deadly to refuse Prince Johnson's invitation. But I could see fear in my brother's face when he left" (Azango 2018).

According to testimony Johnson later provided to Liberia's Truth and Reconciliation Commission, Samuel Varnii, the deputy head of the INPFL, had heard that Tecumsay was gay, and when Tecumsay's arrest came to his attention he ordered a crude, invasive investigation to determine if this was true. "Gen. Varnii ordered Tecumsay Roberts to take off his trouser, and when he took off his trouser, it was discovered that his butt was rotten," Johnson said. "The man whole anus was rotten." After this was over, Varnii ordered that Tecumsay be shot to death.

Sandy Roberts broke down crying when he told *Front-Page Africa* how he learned his brother had been killed. "After two hours of waiting for my brother, I overheard some rebels saying they had just killed a Liberian musician named Tecumsay Roberts," he said, adding that he was told Tecumsay's body had been dumped in a river nearby. "I went along the riverside to look for TR's body but I did not see it."

The details of Tecumsay Roberts' killing have come to define his legacy in the eyes of many Liberians. These days, even among Liberian sexual minorities who might otherwise look to him as an icon, and as a representative

226

of their community's contributions to Liberian cultural life, Roberts is remembered less for how he lived than for how he died.

His death is also seen as encapsulating the general treatment of sexual minorities during the war years, a time when the public became more hostile to them. This was in no small part fueled by the rhetoric of the conflict's primary actors.

The first Liberian war lasted nearly eight years and killed tens of thousands of people. When it finally ended, in 1997, Liberia held a presidential election in which Taylor received 75 percent of the vote, allowing him to claim the prize that he had evidently been fighting for the entire time.

Horton (2012) contends that, after Taylor's inauguration, he employed anti-gay rhetoric to try to remake his image in the eyes of Liberians who saw him only as a combatant. "Taylor the warlord could not reinvent himself as a moral leader, a statesman, without targeting an opposite. If you need to reconstruct yourself like Taylor had to, after so much killing, it serves you well to use a buffer," Horton writes. "He was exceptional, Taylor claimed, not only in contrast to the other warlords he'd outsmarted to seize the presidency; he was also man enough to cleanse the land of walking, breathing abominations."

Anti-gay diatribes from the head of state clearly made Liberian sexual minorities more vulnerable. But even when the fighting was at its peak, Liberia's gay scene didn't disappear entirely, something Patrick witnessed firsthand.

In 1992, a massive battle known as Operation Octopus broke out between rebels who had infiltrated Monrovia and West African peacekeepers that had deployed to secure the city. The intensity of the fighting prompted Patrick to flee the country; he became a refugee in another West African country, where he tried to organize his resettlement in the United States.[1]

A few years later, however, amid a lull in the fighting, he returned to Monrovia to attend his brother's high school graduation. During this brief stay, he reconnected with an old friend, the same security guard who had driven him to the cookout in Airfield a decade earlier. This man was now living with his partner, and the couple hosted private parties for men who slept with men. Patrick attended one, and ended up having sex with a man he met there. Though he had no way of knowing it at the time, it was the last such tryst before he received a diagnosis that would shape the course of the rest of his life.

* * *

Peace finally came to Liberia in 2003. That August, Taylor stepped down and flew to Nigeria, where he had been granted asylum. Two years later, Sirleaf won the country's first postwar presidential election.

As the new government began the monumental task of rebuilding the country, Liberia's community of sexual minorities set about trying to put their own world back together. For most of Sirleaf's first term, they were able to pursue this project in peace—officially unaccepted, as always, but also underground and unmolested. In a country desperate for foreign investment and debt relief, politicians generally avoided the type of anti-LGBT rhetoric that turned off Western officials. Most of the country's citizens, too, had far bigger priorities.

That changed in late 2011 with the publication of the Obama administration's memorandum on LGBT rights and the furor that ensued. Political elites, even those nominally invested in national reconciliation and rehabilitating Liberia's image, revealed a new willingness, even eagerness, to demonize sexual minorities. One of the louder voices in this chorus was Jerome Verdier, the human rights activist who had served as chairman of Liberia's Truth and Reconciliation Commission. In an open letter published by Liberian media outlets in January 2012, Verdier urged Sirleaf's government not to decriminalize same-sex sexual acts. He described homosexuality as "anti-Liberian and anti-God," saying that it was "condemnable as an abomination for the nation." He also warned that "legalizing homosexuality will further erode and degrade the moral fabric of our nation and degenerate its civilization and godliness" (SAIL et al. 2014).

Verdier's references to God and godliness highlight how religion influences Liberian debates about sexual minorities and their place in society. This phenomenon can be seen the world over. Yet in a country where more than 85 percent of the population identifies as Christian, and where Christian leaders have, in recent years, tried to rally public support for amending the constitution to make Liberia a "Christian nation," it can often seem as though religious arguments are fully driving the conversation. At the same time, the specific ways religion operates in Liberia are different from what international observers might expect.

The story of the "Kill the Gays" bill in Uganda has warped outsiders' understanding of how, and by whom, religion is deployed in much of Africa to advance homophobic agendas. In researching the origins of that bill, which was introduced in 2009, Kapya Kaoma (2009/10), a Zambian human rights activist working for Political Research Associates, uncovered the links between leading Ugandan public figures—including the bill's author, David Bahati, a Ugandan lawmaker—and American right-wing evangelicals such as Scott Lively. A purveyor of a decidedly extremist brand of homophobia, Lively has repeatedly described homosexuality as "equivalent to pedophilia, sado-masochism, bestiality and other forms of deviant behavior." In his 1995 book *The Pink Swastika*, he purports to document "the homosexual roots of the Nazi Party" while arguing that "homosexuality figures prominently in the history of the Holocaust." In March 2009, Lively brought these ideas to Uganda, speaking at a "Seminar on Exposing the Homosexuals' Agenda." He later boasted that his appearances in Uganda amounted to a "nuclear bomb" against the "gay agenda" (Southern Poverty Law Center n.d., 2009).

There is little question that Lively and his fellow evangelicals helped create a dangerous environment for Ugandan sexual minorities, one that some Ugandans have said led to the murder of activist David Kato in 2011. In 2012, the organization Sexual Minorities Uganda, or SMUG, in partnership with the Center for Constitutional Rights, filed a lawsuit in the United States against Lively, arguing that his activities in Uganda amounted to persecution. In June 2017, a judge dismissed the case on jurisdictional grounds, though he also stressed that Lively's "crackpot bigotry" had "aided and abetted a vicious and frightening campaign of repression against LGBTI persons in Uganda" (Center for Constitutional Rights 2017).

This type of meddling by Western evangelicals absolutely deserves attention and condemnation. Yet the high-profile nature of the Uganda story, and Lively's role in it, has helped give rise to narratives in which African religious leaders come across as empty vessels with no agency of their own, receptive to whatever white interlopers tell them. It has therefore obscured the other ways in which religious homophobia functions in many African countries.

The Liberian case offers a compelling counternarrative, as the scholars Ashley Currier and Joëlle M. Cruz have demonstrated in their work on the New Citizens Movement, a coalition of Liberian Christian and Muslim leaders that formed in 2012. Muslims make up about 12 percent of Liberia's population, and Currier and Cruz (2017) describe the coalition as an example of how public debate about LGBT rights had "reinvigorated a Christian–Muslim alliance that dates back to efforts to end the civil war."

Though the New Citizens Movement was ostensibly trying to address "social crises" in general, its early work was devoted almost exclusively to combating the dangers presented by alternative sexualities. As part of a campaign against gay rights, and specifically against any push for the legalization of same-sex marriage, it launched a drive to collect 100,000 signatures on a petition urging Sirleaf to keep the government's laws concerning same-sex sexual acts in place.

The New Citizens Movement did not receive outside funding, nor did it appear to benefit from the kind of foreign connections that Ugandan religious and political leaders did. Moreover, in making its case to the public, the coalition fashioned arguments reflecting specifically Liberian concerns. Claiming that Liberians overwhelmingly rejected LGBT rights, spokespeople for the New Citizens Movement warned that any move to expand them could force the country back into conflict, undermining the gains of a decade of peace. And when pushing the well-worn line about alternative sexualities endangering the country's youth, they invoked the country's fragile economy and young people's struggle to find work. For example, Cleopatra Watson, a leader of the New Citizens Movement, told me in an interview that she knew many qualified young job applicants who had been denied work because of their refusal to engage in same-sex sexual acts with people who might hire them.

While highly unlikely, this was a savvy talking point that served the interests of Liberian elites. High unemployment in Liberia, like everywhere else, is bruising to a country's psyche. It suggests that schools aren't effectively educating students, that the government is failing to attract investment, and that Liberian businesspeople are not competing at the same level as their peers elsewhere in the region. In short, it is a condemnation of those in charge. It would therefore be convenient if the problem could be blamed on a small minority group that, while altogether powerless, somehow has the ability to put a stranglehold on the economy.

Rather than being pushed by foreigners, then, in this case religious homophobia was wielded by Liberians who deliberately played on domestic concerns to render it as potent as possible. This dynamic may not have been immediately apparent to outside observers, but Liberian sexual minorities, in many cases, read it accurately from the beginning.

These activists also recognized something else: that the indigenous roots of religious homophobia didn't necessarily make it more of a threat. To the contrary, as Sirleaf's second term progressed, they showed how it could be effectively countered with a little resistance.

13

Let that awareness be created

Patrick didn't stay long in Liberia. After spending a few days in Monrovia attending the ceremonies and parties organized in honor of his brother's graduation, he got back on the road and returned to the West African country where he had been living with other Liberian refugees. His plan—his only ambition, really—was to continue trying to relocate to the United States.

Shortly after his return, though, Patrick fell sick. One morning, he awoke with a burning pain on one side of his body, and he discovered that he had developed a rash. When he went to a United Nations-run clinic, he learned that he had shingles. After undergoing other tests, he received an additional diagnosis: He was HIV-positive.

Patrick is not sure how he contracted the virus. It could have happened while he was still in Monrovia or after he left. In the end, the details mattered little compared to what the diagnosis meant for his future: Other Liberian refugees told him that it effectively nixed any chance he would be granted a US visa. All the time he'd spent sitting for interviews and trying to get his papers in order had amounted, it seemed, to nothing.

Going to America was the one thing Patrick had been looking forward to. Now that it seemed out of reach, he became so despondent that he remembers thinking he didn't want to live anymore. He decided to return to Liberia, but he had no idea what he would do there. Before making the trip, he sent a letter to the headquarters of the UN refugee agency in Geneva. He explained his situation, and stated that his plan was, essentially, to go back to Monrovia and wait for AIDS to kill him.

Once back home, Patrick spent long, aimless days doing just that. The apartment where he stayed, in the city center, was across the street from a brothel, and when he looked out the window he could see sex workers negotiating with clients before inviting them inside. He assumed they probably had as little information about HIV/AIDS and other sexually transmitted illnesses as he had been given before he became sexually active. The thought of what might happen to them if they were to become sick, and the lack of resources that would be at their disposal, made him despair even further.

Patrick describes this period as among the lowest of his life. But it didn't last more than a few months. Soon, Patrick received a different, happier surprise. The letter he had sent to Geneva had somehow ended up in the hands of an official at UNAIDS. This official managed to reach him in Monrovia and introduced him to a representative of an American nonprofit organization. As a result of this introduction, Patrick received a grant of $5,000 to come up with a project to help address the lack of prevention and treatment services for HIV/AIDS in Liberia. Patrick would use this money to help found Stop AIDS in Liberia, or SAIL, the organization that quickly took over his life.

* * *

SAIL was the first organization created by and for Liberian sexual minorities. For the first decade and a half of its existence, it remained decidedly small-scale, guided by a narrow focus on the day-to-day work of providing HIV/AIDS-related services to high-risk populations, principally men who have sex with men. Its members tried to test as many of these men as possible, and to provide counseling for those whose results came back positive. They also volunteered at a clinic in Monrovia, serving as caregivers to those who were struggling to access treatment.

One of the main factors that prevented SAIL from scaling up its operations in the early years was a lack of available funding, a problem compounded by Patrick's limited experience in navigating donor networks. By all accounts, SAIL was wholly unprepared when, in 2012, seemingly out of nowhere, LGBT rights became a subject of national discussion in Liberia. It had just seven staff members, all of them MSM, working in a cramped office in downtown Monrovia that offered no security.

As the environment became increasingly hostile, members of SAIL concentrated on keeping themselves and other sexual minorities safe. With the help of organizations like ActionAid, a human rights and anti-poverty NGO whose local chapter was, at the time, headed by the Liberian feminist activist Korto Williams, they held security training sessions to get members of the community thinking about how to avoid threatening situations and how to react if they inadvertently ended up in one. In the early months of 2012, as lawmakers considered draft legislation criminalizing same-sex marriage and imposing harsher penalties for same-sex sexual acts, this type of activism seemed to them to be the most valuable. As underscored by President Sirleaf's paean to traditional values in her interview with *The Guardian*, Patrick and his peers weren't likely to get anywhere by lobbying the government directly (Ford and Allen 2012).

Four months after that interview was published, the Liberian Senate approved Jewel Howard Taylor's bill criminalizing gay marriage. Yet that was as far as any of the proposed anti-LGBT legislation advanced. The bills never reached Sirleaf's desk—perhaps because she had told *The*

Guardian that she would not sign "any law that has to do with that area"—meaning they did not become law. Eventually, in the press and among the political class, the debate over LGBT rights died down, and activists seized this moment to mount a quiet counteroffensive.

Their ability to do this was significantly enhanced by the very development that had initially made them vulnerable: the State Department's decision to promote the human rights of sexual minorities overseas. Though this news had prompted a violent backlash, it had also greatly increased the level of interest in and funding available for the type of work carried out by SAIL. Additionally, after the initial furor passed, it empowered groups like SAIL to be more proactive in their outreach to government officials and in their attempts to build alliances with other civil society organizations. In a country where the US Embassy wields an inordinate amount of influence, the fact that they ostensibly had Washington's support gave them a sense of security they didn't have before.

As they grew bolder, Patrick and his activist peers began reaching out to new constituencies. To counter negative press coverage of Liberian sexual minorities, including articles blaming them for the fact that HIV/AIDS was present in the country at all, they contacted journalists directly, despite the threat of blackmail and violence. In late 2013, they distributed a report to journalists that had been produced in partnership with Human Rights Watch (2013) explaining how talk of new anti-LGBT legislation had "already exacerbated discrimination, harassment and stigmatization."

New, unexpected voices turned out to be receptive to this message. One day in 2012, journalist Necus Andrews happened upon SAIL's offices and walked in to introduce himself. The previous year, Andrews had founded an organization called the Anti-AIDS Media Network, a group of around twenty-five journalists interested in improving how Liberian media outlets covered news affecting people living with HIV/AIDS. He thought he had met almost everyone working on HIV/AIDS issues since then, but he had never heard of SAIL. Nor did he have any understanding of the lives of MSM in Liberia. This is despite the fact, that, according to a 2013 study conducted by UNAIDS, the prevalence rate among MSM in Liberia is 19.8 percent, compared to 2.1 percent for the general population. "This is a country where those issues are still taboo," Andrews says. "When you are growing up, all you hear is that gay people are sinners going against God's will, that they are individuals who don't deserve life."

He decided to start bringing MSM to his organization's training sessions. He encouraged Liberian journalists to file balanced stories about sexual minorities, and he has tried to do that himself for his newspaper, *The News*, regardless of the sometimes uncomfortable scrutiny he receives from his editors. "In my newsroom, every time they see stories from me about HIV/AIDS and key populations, they say, 'Are you an advocate for gays?' And I say, 'What does that mean? Am I not a journalist?' My profession tells me that I should report beyond borders. If a man says he is MSM and he's been violated, should I close my eyes to that?"

As part of this new partnership, SAIL and the Anti-AIDS Media Network produced a guide for journalists looking to report more responsibly on people affected by HIV/AIDS. Patrick says it is just one example of a broader effort to soften public discourse related to sexual minorities—an effort he believes has gradually created space for a wider range of views. "There's more dialogue," he says, reflecting on how public discussion of the issue has changed. "There isn't as much violence at the level of personal attacks and all of that."

The potential for this dialogue to cultivate still more allies was on display at a workshop organized by Liberian LGBT activists in early 2017 at ActionAid's offices. Most of the programming involved activists describing, before an audience of law enforcement officials and representatives of other civil society groups, various abuses they had suffered. In many cases, they offered detailed accounts of physical attacks, including sexual violence. Afterward, those in attendance were invited to share their thoughts and ask questions.

Many of the comments were simple statements of gratitude to those who had been willing to share their stories. One woman, a representative of a Christian NGO, said this kind of event could help tear down some of the remaining stigma that clings to Liberian sexual minorities.

It was a process, she said, that reminded her of how perceptions of women with HIV/AIDS in Liberia had evolved. Though such women were once treated as pariahs, they had managed to convince Liberian society that their diagnosis was no reason to fear them or exclude them from their communities.

This remark was followed by a comment from a representative of the Liberia National Police, a force that sexual minorities had long been conditioned to fear. He, too, thanked those sexual minorities who had spoken, and he described with apparent conviction his desire to know more about their lives and how the police force might better serve them.

"We pray that every time you notice a violation—not just against you, but any of the community members—please notify our nearest police station," the officer said. "If you feel that the police station doesn't act, we have a way of creating a sense of redress to handle that issue. Because human rights now, in our department, it's something that we subscribe to, it's something that we recognize."

He continued: "You know, we are not so much schooled in the human rights issues and the various sexual identity issues. Let that awareness be created. Let the experts that have the skills come and teach our people these things, because knowledge is power. Once our people are informed, we don't believe we can stop these violations, no, but we can help to minimize them."

* * *

The movement Patrick helped create has, in recent years, grown to be much bigger than SAIL and the men it serves. At least five other organizations have formed to work on behalf of various constituencies within Liberia's sexual minority milieu. There are now multiple groups that work exclusively with lesbian and bisexual women, and another created for transgender women. These groups are new and glaringly underfunded, but other activists take them seriously. If nothing else, they succeed in providing safe spaces for Liberians who otherwise would be on their own.

Their leaders have also become skilled at taking advantage of the support foreign embassies provide. American diplomats, in particular, have proved to be a consistent source of low-profile encouragement, offering to send representatives to court cases involving community members who run into trouble with the police; to make Embassy facilities available for the groups' activities; and to raise the concerns of LGBT Liberians with government officials.

Meanwhile, SAIL itself has expanded significantly. In 2016, the organization moved into a much larger building in Monrovia's Mamba Point neighborhood, a stone's throw from the ocean. Its staff had quadrupled to twenty-eight, in no small part because its income had expanded significantly. Whereas previously the funds SAIL received were earmarked almost exclusively for HIV/AIDS programming, today about half a dozen groups, most of which are based in the US, finance SAIL's work in both public health and human rights. This backing has helped make SAIL's programming somewhat more inclusive, serving lesbian and bisexual women and transgender Liberians.

One person who has benefited from this is Fatu, a Liberian woman who began working at SAIL as the office manager in 2015. She describes the job as something that fell into her lap by word of mouth. Prior to SAIL, she had been working as a volunteer at a girls' school.

Fatu's work days at SAIL are consumed by the unflashy but essential tasks that keep the organization running: She oversees maintenance of computers and other technology. She makes sure the office has a steady supply of water and electricity. She goes to the bank to withdraw money to pay staff.

All the while, the job has given her a chance to grow more at ease in her own skin. As recently as 2014, Fatu concealed her attraction to women from everyone except close friends. For many years, she had dated men, though her flirtations and periodic trysts with women inevitably complicated things. She told her last boyfriend, for instance, that she was bisexual, but that she "wasn't involved anymore." But in Monrovia, a city so small there is no space for secrets, he learned within a few months that this was a lie. "He texted me and he said, 'You know, I've been hearing about you, your involvement with same-sex, and I can't continue. I can't keep seeing you, and we should stay apart,'" Fatu recalls. "So yeah, he broke up with me because of my sexuality."

Fatu was upset about this, but only to a point. She acknowledges that a large part of the relationship's appeal was that it deflected attention from those who wonder why she rarely wears dresses or is seen on the arm of a man. Asked if she was genuinely attracted to her ex-boyfriend, she responds diplomatically. "Um, he's a nice person," she says. "I think a little bit, yeah, I was attracted to him a little bit. But honestly if I was in another country where it's legal, I would only date women."

The job with SAIL didn't take her to another country, but it did invite her into a small, self-contained world in which her attraction to women was seen as completely natural, and something she was encouraged to discuss. "When I'm here, I'm free to talk about how I spend the night with a girl, or maybe relationship stuff," she says.

> I feel free. The people, they make it easy for you to know yourself, to know who you are exactly and not be afraid and not feel like you are left out or alone in this. Especially Patrick. He talks to you. He encourages you to fight harder for your dreams. What you want to do, you have to push through. He always supports people.

As she has grown comfortable within the walls of SAIL's headquarters, Fatu has also, on occasion, become brave enough to apply these lessons outside them. This was the case during an incident that took place in early 2017 at

Sajj House, a Lebanese restaurant in Monrovia's Sinkor neighborhood.

Friday nights at Sajj have, for several years now, been a draw for expats and upper-class Liberians alike. For a few hours each week, a place that typically offers little more than shawarma and bland pizza served beneath overhead fans transforms into an ad hoc dance club, loud and sweaty, with a DJ in an elevated booth mixing the Hot 100 with a dash of Trace Africa's Top 10.

Fatu headed out to Sajj with three friends, including a younger girl, a high school student, with whom she had been flirting for several weeks. When she has a few drinks, Fatu tends to police her public behavior less vigorously, and on this particular night she began, in the middle of the crowd, to dance closely with her crush. Before long, she noticed she had attracted the attention of several people nearby, including a man who appeared to be filming her with his phone.

Emboldened by beer, Fatu confronted the man. "I said, 'Do you know me? Why would you take a video of me? We're not even friends!'" she recalls. The man denied recording anything, but Fatu snatched the phone out of his hand and immediately opened Snapchat, where she found two clips of herself from just moments earlier. One of them had already been posted. The second was still a draft. For a caption, the man had written, "This is what is happening in our country."

Now Fatu was angry. Taking the man's phone with her, she walked over to the Sajj security guards and played the clip for them. The guards approached the man. "I had the feeling to, you know, break his phone or even seize it," Fatu says, "but then they talked to me and they told me to just delete it and give it back to him, and they would put him outside." Sure enough, the guards, invoking a rule against filming other customers, threw the man out on the street. No mention was made of the fact that Fatu had been dancing with another woman.

In bird's-eye surveys of LGBT liberation movements, individual acts of defiance such as Fatu's—the countless confrontations, large and small, that activists engage in day after day—don't generally merit a mention. These narratives instead foreground high-profile showdowns: police raids, attacks on prominent activists, courtroom victories.

Yet when stories like Fatu's multiply and build upon each other, they can signify momentous change. At the same time, the true depth and durability of this change may only be truly perceptible in a time of crisis.

Fatu and her fellow activists would not need to wait long before such a crisis presented itself. As it happened, in the lead-up to Liberia's 2017 presidential election, their humanity, and their basic rights, would once again be put up for debate.

14

Grown woman

SAIL's evolution over the past few years, from an organization focused on men who have sex with men to one that aims to serve all Liberian sexual minorities, has forced Patrick and his colleagues to grapple with issues that, for decades, they could get away with ignoring. Unsurprisingly, their biggest blind spots have involved issues specific to women. By their own admission, it is only recently that they have paid much attention to how sexism functions in Liberian society, and to the difficulties women and girls face trying to educate themselves, find jobs and build lives that don't revolve around men.

In Fatu's view, SAIL's leaders have risen to the challenge, in part by giving more opportunities to the growing number of women, herself included, in their ranks. In general, she finds that SAIL's male and female members have more in common than not. "We like the same thing, so we can better understand each other when it comes to relationships and, you know, giving advice," she says. "You would understand because you're with the same sex and I'm with the same sex, so working together is not difficult."

There are advantages to having an organization composed of both men and women. One of the most important is the fact that they can socialize together, and take up space in public together, more easily than an organization composed exclusively of lesbians and bisexual women. Fatu sometimes makes a show of flirting with SAIL's male members in public to throw people off. "I'm friends with the guys and we can talk, we can hang out," she says. "If we hang out, I have to be all over them, because I can't be all over a girl."

Yet for some sexual minorities in Liberia, the benefits of SAIL's inclusiveness are outweighed by the feeling that their own, unique interests are still sidelined, meaning they remain marginalized even within a movement of marginalized people. This was the precise sentiment that prompted a young Liberian activist named Karishma to branch off and form her own organization in 2014.

All her life, Karishma had an aversion to the male identity she was given at birth, and to the male name her parents and other relatives called her by. Well before she became aware of her sexual attraction to men, she knew that she was female, even if no one around her could see it. "People used to recognize me as, 'Oh, you sissy boy,' like a fag," she recalls. "But I knew who I was. I knew that I was different."

In 2003, when Karishma was thirteen, her family, angered by what they perceived as Karishma's stubborn unwillingness to conform, kicked her out of the house. Karishma spent the next six years supporting herself as a sex worker on the streets of postwar Monrovia. When she wasn't spending the night with clients, she slept on the beach or in unfinished or abandoned buildings.

As she approached twenty, she decided that she needed to resume her studies and finish her education, which had been cut short when she became homeless. "I'm a very optimistic person," she says. "I had to do everything to make life possible."

She also began making inroads in Liberia's community of sexual minorities, eventually connecting with Patrick and other members of SAIL. It was 2010, and many activists, both within and outside Liberia, seemed to be engaging with issues related to gender identity for the first time. Though Karishma was not yet referring to herself as trans-gender, she found that her story had a certain currency she hadn't expected, especially with foreigners.

Within a few years, by dint of some savvy networking, she had managed to transform herself into what Liberian activists call—sometimes with respect, sometimes with jealousy and disdain—a "travel diva": a regular on the global LGBT rights conference circuit. On panels and over dinners in hotels in foreign capitals, she was often asked to describe for American and European donors the challenges faced by Liberian sexual minorities, and how well-meaning outsiders might help.

But the transfer of knowledge went both ways. While attending meetings and pursuing internships in places like London, Johannesburg and Bangkok, Karishma, who had educated herself on transgender issues online, met and befriended transgender activists from other countries, learning in the process what the word is generally taken to mean and how it is generally lived. Though wary of the identity in the beginning, having first encountered it while reading an article about a transgender woman who was murdered in Los Angeles, she ultimately concluded that she fully identified with it, and that it answered outstanding questions about who she was. Since then, she has been working toward building a transgender community in her own country.

Karishma named her new group the Transgender Network of Liberia, or TNOL. "We felt it was important to have our own organization because we saw the need," she says. "I took it from my standpoint, from being a child who wakes up in the morning, I look in the mirror and see this beautiful, flawless face, but within the community people were identifying me as male, and I didn't know who I was." She adds, "I said to myself that there's going to come a time when there are people who are going to be like me, who are going to identify like me." She wanted these people to have somewhere to turn.

The timing worked in her favor. Patrick says TNOL's founding coincided with a new willingness on the part of members of Liberia's LGBT community to speak more openly about their questions concerning gender identity. "Every single person has a story," he says.

> I listen to all of their stories, every day, and I try to put it together and it just, like, it blows my mind. Because someone will come and say, "Patrick, I've never felt like I'm a man. I always felt like I was trapped." I have the conversation and in my mind I'm thinking, "How many of these families, how many mothers and fathers are having these conversations with their kids?"

Karishma's mission with TNOL—to create a space where those conversations can happen, and where transgender Liberians can explore their identities—is complicated, to say the least. In a country where any kind of gender nonconformity carries a high risk of violence and police harassment, to present as a gender other than the gender everyone understands you to be is often unthinkable. Many of Liberia's trans women therefore present as male much of the time, with the primary exceptions being TNOL meetings and private parties. Even those brief respites from social restrictions come with considerable risk.

On a Sunday night in November 2016, around 100 Liberian sexual minorities gathered on a stretch of beach outside Monrovia for an event organized by TNOL to mark Transgender Day of Remembrance. For Karishma, the program had two somewhat discordant objectives: to honor transgender Liberians who had died in 2016, and to introduce candidates for the 2017 Miss Trans Diva pageant, one of the community's most important, and most high-spirited, annual parties.

The evening began with a moment of silence. But as soon as that ended, the up-tempo beat of Beyoncé's 2013 hit "Grown Woman" came through the speakers, and the pageant's seven contestants began their first passes down the red carpet that had been spread over the wooden stage. Over the next few hours, each woman modeled three outfits—casual wear, evening wear and bright Liberian lappa prints, or "traditional" wear—as the audience danced and drank Club Beer, the more intoxicated among them jokingly shouting proposals of marriage. Though this was only a warm-up event for the actual pageant, after midnight a panel of judges selected the evening's "winner," who was presented with a pink-and-blue cake.

Security guards had been hired for the event, but they left as soon as it was over. Karishma and her friends, along with many of the other guests, stayed long after that. The space they had rented is private and fenced off, but it sits along a stretch of beach that everyone can access. There are also homes nearby, and residents of the neighborhood are known for their hostility to sexual minorities who attend parties there. "This community is noted for very bad things," says Fatu, who attended the pageant but left shortly after it ended. "They are noted to be very disgruntled."

At around 4 a.m., some partygoers decided it was time to leave. One attendee, a Ghanaian man named Kwame, remembers urging them to stay until it was light outside, so that it would be safer for them to get back to the main road. "We told them it's too early because the people who live in that environment, the guys are very rude," he says. The winner of the pageant, however, insisted on leaving, and walked out with her cake in hand, along with her mother and boyfriend.

The party had probably already attracted attention. But as soon as the neighborhood's residents saw the cake, they started crying out that the event was, in fact, a gay wedding. Armed with knives, machetes and sticks, a group of them chased the winner and her entourage back onto the private section of the beach, and then began threatening to attack everyone there. "We want to kill the gay people here. They're going to spoil our kids," one witness remembers the assailants saying. Another witness, a member of TNOL who was involved in organizing the pageant, says that some of them seemed to take particular issue with the fact that transgender Liberians were involved. "When they came back on the beach, the people said, 'Oh, you guys, you are fine guys who decided to be women, come back on the beach I'm going to fuck you'—excuse me for my expression—'I'm going to use stick on you.'"

There were more than twenty-five partygoers still hanging around at that point, and they gathered inside a structure on the private beach, huddling in fear. The assailants tried to enter, rattling the locked doors and windows, trapping the partygoers for several hours. "They said if one person comes outside they will kill you," Kwame remembers.

It was the LGBT activist community's contacts with law enforcement that eventually enabled them to defuse the situation. Someone managed to place a call to Patrick, who then called commanders with the Liberia National Police. Police officers soon arrived on the scene, where they were immediately met with opposition from the residents. "When the police came," Kwame says, "the community even jumped on the police, started fighting the police, saying 'Oh, you guys are promoting this thing in Liberia. It will not hold. This is not America.'"

The police officers took statements and invited residents to file criminal complaints if they had seen anything illegal. But they also admonished them not to threaten or attack members of the community. By mid-morning, they had managed to disperse the crowd, escorting Karishma and her friends to safety.

* * *

Perhaps the most remarkable aspect of the Miss Trans Diva pageant is that, just a few years before it was held, none of the contestants would have referred to themselves as transgender; only a few of them had even heard the word.

According to many of TNOL's members, it is thanks solely to Karishma that they have assumed this new identity.

The experience of Harmony, an early member of TNOL, tracks with Karishma's in important ways. From a young age, her family, assuming she was a gay man, treated her with hostility. When she was a teenager, her older brother decided that they could no longer live in the same house. He poisoned Harmony's food, sending her to the hospital, a fact he openly acknowledged when confronted by their mother. "He said it was because I choose to be gay, and he hates gays and wants to get rid of me," Harmony says. Her father, it turned out, also wanted to get rid of her, so she was kicked out of the family home. To survive, she resorted to sex work in Liberia and in neighboring Ghana, where she lived for a time.

Since then, her older sister and her mother have reached out to her and offered to take her back in. But while her father is dead, her older brother is still around, and her sister's boyfriend is intensely homophobic, too. "This boyfriend is a threat to my life," Harmony says. "He says I'm a gay, I cannot be in the same house where he is. He threatens to disgrace me publicly. He even used the statement that if I'm in the same house with him, it will lead to my death." So Harmony has to settle with meeting her mother in restaurants, without the rest of the family knowing.

Harmony met Karishma several years ago, and they talked frequently as Karishma educated herself on trans issues. It was, naturally, Karishma who first told Harmony what the word transgender means. "Transgender has to do with someone being born in the wrong body," Harmony says. "For a male born with a female characteristic, who feels like a woman from her expression and attitude, and for a female born with a male character." Harmony identified with the word immediately, and joined TNOL as soon as it formed.

Mekella, another member, has faced less resistance from her family as she's explored her identity. Growing up, her siblings and father tried to treat her as a boy, but she clung to her mother, helping her with the cooking and cleaning and doing other tasks typically assigned to little girls. Though her mother also considered her to be a boy, and to this day calls her by the male name she was given at birth, she also proved to be a dependable ally, protecting Mekella from those, including her father, who might otherwise be more abusive.

Her mother has also signaled her acceptance in other ways. In Nigerian and Liberian films, a common comedic trope is to have a man dress up disguised as a woman, often poorly, with messy makeup and ridiculous wigs. Mekella's mother loves these films, and sometimes she calls Mekella over to watch them. "She says, 'The way you act is just like that movie. Do you want to be like that girl?'" When Mekella says yes, her mother simply nods.

More recently, the family has gotten used to other members of TNOL coming by the family home. Greeting them at the door, her mother will say, "Your sister is just inside." She has also teased Mekella about her many boyfriends, saying that she needs to bring them over so they can be introduced to the family.

This kind of talk can be too much for her father. "He says, 'The day I find it out, he will leave my house,'" Mekella says. But her mother never fails to shut down those threats. "She says, 'No, he grew up around women. That's why he acts like that.'"

Even though she's been given some space at home to explore who she is, Mekella says she would never have developed a full understanding of her identity, or learned the word transgender, if she hadn't decided to attend one of Karishma's workshops one day in 2016. Like other members of TNOL, she also credits Karishma with showing her how to be safe in Monrovia, how to police her behavior so as not to attract unnecessary scrutiny.

According to Beyoncé, one of TNOL's newer members, one of the greatest benefits of joining the organization has been having an outlet to show, via her clothing and how she acts at TNOL-organized functions, that she is different from gay men. "Especially when we are in a gathering, we want to show that we are a typical woman," she says. "Like wearing a woman's outfit, talking, sashaying."

But Karishma has also taught her that she can only do these things in certain spaces. On an ordinary weekday, heading into TNOL's offices, Beyoncé wears jeans, a T-shirt, loafers, maybe a denim jacket—all things that a man would wear. She is confident that when she's out on the street, or in a share-taxi, Liberians assume she is a man. "I dress according to the kind of society I find myself in," she says.

It can be difficult to remember when to keep this mask on and when to let it slip. "Sometimes I'll be talking, and the time comes that I'll lose control," Beyoncé says. "When I see too many eyes coming back on me, I'll say, 'Oh, I have to come back.' I have to position myself and keep the border right."

TNOL members say the fact that hormone therapy, to say nothing of gender-affirmation surgery, is not available in Liberia makes it easier for them to present as male when they need to. While some members are unequivocal in their desire to follow in Karishma's shoes and go abroad for this kind of treatment, others are more conflicted, especially those, like Mekella, who retain ties to their families.

Mekella doesn't know how she could possibly return from undergoing hormone therapy and be welcomed at home. "This is one of the difficult decisions you will take, because you will not be the kind of person you were before," she says.

If I have changed myself with everything, I will not be coming back to wear the same outfits I used to wear. I will not be coming with that again. I'll be changing my hair, making my hair longer. I will work on everything. I will be totally different, because I want to be a woman, so why would I still be wearing a man's outfit?

She continues: "If I go to my parents' house and say, 'It's me, Mekella,' they'd say, 'Who?' So this is something that, if you are doing it, you have to be established. You have to be someone who has everything on your own."

The fact that many of TNOL's members are, for the time being, often mistaken for men is a source of tension between them and other Liberian sexual minorities. Some gay and bisexual men, especially, suspect TNOL's members are gay men themselves, and that they have simply fallen under the spell of Karishma, perhaps because they want their share of the resources, however paltry, that are increasingly available for transgender organizing. In a country as poor as Liberia, this kind of resentment, like the flack Karishma catches for her frequent travels, is perhaps inevitable.

Yet those who have actually spent time with TNOL's members believe the work they're doing is necessary. Cyriaque, an Ivorian activist who works frequently with activists in Liberia, says Karishma's workshops are conducted in a way that helps participants better understand themselves. "Everyone who has participated in these sessions, the feedback has been very positive," he says. "A lot of people who are trans were calling themselves MSM. After the workshop, they say, 'I think I am trans, I'm not MSM.' But they've also understood that trans is not simply putting on a dress. It's really something that you think in your head."

* * *

Karishma has become used to brushing off criticism as she focuses on building her movement. At the same time, she has tried to lead something of a balanced life, including cultivating her relationship with Kwame, whom she started dating after they met in a nightclub a few years ago.

Kwame had been in Monrovia for just a few weeks at that point. Born in Ghana, he had followed his mother and sister over the border the previous year, but he had spent most of his time in Grand Gedeh, in southeastern Liberia, where his sister worked as a beautician. In Monrovia, he was staying with an older man he had met at a church in Grand Gedeh. He didn't know what he was going to do with himself in the capital, or how long he would be staying.

He remembers being taken with Karishma from the moment he saw her enter the nightclub. He went up and introduced himself. "It was late, I was leaving. I was drunk. I was hungry. I don't know what came over me, I just went directly to her. I didn't know her, she didn't know me," he says. "I went to her, I said, 'Hello, can you please help me to buy something to eat?' She said, 'No problem, I don't have money but I will go home and come.' I said OK. When she came she bought me fried egg, bread and energy drink."

As the two got to talking, Kwame became even more intrigued. "You know how she likes to act, going around," he says, smiling. "And actually, I like the way she moves, the way she walks, the way she dances, stuff like that. Even the way she speaks, loud and direct, I just love it."

They soon started dating, and eventually they moved in together in a ground-floor apartment in Mamba Point. As the relationship progressed, Kwame became interested in her activism, and also in examining his own sexual orientation. He says that before meeting Karishma, he identified as bisexual. These days, he says he's "attracted to men, 100 percent," even though Karishma identifies as a woman. He says that if Karishma were to undergo gender-affirmation surgery, it "wouldn't change anything" in their relationship, and that he would continue to identify as gay.

Their dynamic is an example of how labels, in their inflexibility, fail to capture the complexity of individual lives. At the end of the day, Kwame thinks less about how he identifies than about his specific relationship. This is all the more true now that the two refer to themselves as a married couple, having gone through an ad hoc ceremony in 2016.

The wedding was Kwame's idea, though Karishma says she was instantly on board. "One of the main reasons I got married to her is because she is very educated," Kwame says. "I would say she is talented, yeah, I saw all those things in her that really encouraged me to get married to her."

For the ceremony, dozens of guests gathered at a private compound in Monrovia. Those in attendance included friends and fellow activists, as well as some family members. Karishma had two of her sisters there. Kwame had two of his brothers as well as an uncle, a pastor who officiated.

The crowd sat on plastic chairs facing the altar. Before the ceremony started, Kwame stood at the altar by himself, wearing a long-sleeve white shirt, a sky blue vest and a sky blue bowtie.

Beyoncé's "Grown Woman" came through the speakers as heads turned to watch Karishma make her entrance. She wore more or less the same outfit as Kwame, though she had on a necktie instead of a bowtie, and she had fashioned a piece of blue fabric into a train that ran behind her. "I'm a grown woman, I can do whatever I want," Beyoncé could be heard singing as Karishma walked down the aisle.

Then it was time for the couple to exchange vows. "I told him whether in sickness or not, I would always love him," Karishma says. "Whether he's rich or poor I would always love him, and regardless of if there is a meal on the table or no meal on the table, I'm going to love him, in the rain, in the sun, I'm always going to love him, and I accept to be his wife till death do us part."

To which Kwame responded: "From the day I saw you, I always knew you were my wife. I don't think I can stop loving you ... I'm proud of who you are and I'm proud of who I am."

15

Finding our
own champions

In early August 2016, Prince Johnson, the former rebel leader, launched his second campaign for the Liberian presidency. To his supporters, it was to be the capstone of a public transformation that had once seemed all but impossible.

Outside Liberia, Johnson will forever be associated primarily with events that took place nearly three decades ago, on a Sunday in September 1990. A former officer in the Armed Forces of Liberia, he had been an early supporter of Charles Taylor, commanding his elite Special Forces unit after the first civil war began in 1989. Within months, however, Johnson split off to form his own group, which eventually took over parts of Monrovia, including the port.

On September 9, 1990, Samuel Doe, the president whom the rebels were trying to overthrow, left Monrovia's

Executive Mansion to travel to the port, where a West African peacekeeping force was also based. During a meeting between Doe and the peacekeepers' commander, Lieutenant-General Arnold Quainoo of Ghana, Johnson's heavily armed fighters showed up and initiated one of the most fateful skirmishes of the entire conflict.

Overpowering Doe's men, the rebels took the president into custody and presented him to Johnson. Video footage of what followed would later become widely available on the streets of Monrovia and elsewhere in West Africa. It shows Johnson, sitting behind a desk, drinking a Budweiser as a woman fans him. Johnson barks questions at Doe while other rebels torture him, ignoring the president's pleas to spare his life. At one point, Johnson orders his men to slice off Doe's ear, which they do. According to some reports, Johnson then proceeded to eat part of the ear. Johnson himself has boasted, "I cut off his ears made him eat them." In any case, Doe did not live through the night.

These images trail Johnson to this day, but, to many Liberians, they do not define him. In a country that has never held criminal prosecutions for wartime atrocities, Johnson has not had to answer for Doe's killing. This has allowed him to reinvent himself, first by declaring himself a born-again Christian, then by pursuing a political career that, in the words of the International Crisis Group (2011), is "incongruously based on his wartime record and security credentials."

In the 2005 general elections, Johnson became a senator representing Nimba County, whose residents still praise him for defending them after the fighting broke out. He followed this up with a presidential bid in 2011. He came in third place in the first round that year, earning 11.4 percent of the vote, and his endorsement of President Sirleaf in the runoff is credited with helping her secure a second term.

His second presidential run was to be broadly animated by the same themes that shaped the first: Johnson presented himself to voters as the candidate best placed to root out corruption and champion the interests of indigenous Liberians.

But he also added a new element, which he unveiled during his campaign kickoff event in August 2016 in Monrovia. "The government, under our watch, will never, ever accept gay rights. Liberia is not Sodom and Gomorrah," Johnson told his assembled supporters. "We will never accept that here. I want the West to take note of that and get me clearly" (Corey-Boulet 2016).

These words seemed largely out of sync with the concerns of a nation still recovering from the West African Ebola epidemic, which had killed more than 4,800 people in Liberia alone, threatening to undo the gains of more than a decade of postwar recovery. Nevertheless, they led the coverage of the first weeks of Johnson's campaign, overshadowing his vows to boost the salaries of teachers and health workers and to "jealously guard the peace."

With just a few short statements, Johnson had managed, however briefly, to re-center LGBT rights in the national conversation, and the issue soon threatened to dominate the entire election cycle. Other candidates began fielding questions from journalists on LGBT rights and same-sex marriage, and *FrontPage Africa* described LGBT rights as one of the major issues "that could or should decide" who would become the next president (Sieh 2016).

In turning the public's attention to issues concerning sexual minorities, Johnson had help from outsiders. Three months after his campaign launch, in November 2016, Justin Trudeau, the Canadian prime minister, visited Liberia for a series of meetings and a joint press conference with Sirleaf. The official purpose of the visit was for the two leaders "to discuss issues of mutual interest," notably security issues, gender equality and economic growth. But a member of the Canadian press corps, perhaps seeking something more headline-worthy, asked Trudeau for his thoughts on widespread opposition in Liberia to same-sex marriage, which has been legal in Canada since 2005.

In his response, Trudeau seemed determined not to take an especially confrontational stand, or to contrast himself too sharply with Sirleaf. "The fact is countries have different paces of evolution in terms of recognizing and enshrining those rights, but we can see that there has been tremendous progress over the years in many different areas," he said. "I know that President Sirleaf has taken very strong and clear leadership on the issue of female genital mutilation, which is something that is extremely important when you want to talk about giving women and girls full rights and full opportunity to succeed."

He added, "I understand culture can be a challenge in pushing that, but doing the right thing is something that people shouldn't shy away from, and I truly commend Madame President for her tremendous leadership on that and on many issues" (CBC News 2016).

These statements brought Trudeau some criticism at home, including from Canada's New Democratic Party, which argued that he should have been more forceful in his defense of sexual minorities. Liberian journalists, though, seemed more interested in Sirleaf's response. Apparently having learned from her joint interview with Tony Blair for *The Guardian* several years earlier, she kept things as benign as possible, eschewing any mention of traditional values and instead claiming that Liberia "has no law that restricts the rights of individuals to their own choices." She added, "Only when it is a threat to national security do we have a law that has restrictions. The freedom of choice is extended to all Liberians." Various Liberian media outlets noted the shift in tone, and speculated that it could reflect a shift in policy.

Given the longstanding ban on voluntary sodomy in Liberia, what Sirleaf said wasn't exactly true. Liberian sexual minorities defended her anyway. One member of SAIL, George, described her statement as a welcome softening of what she had said during Blair's visit in 2012, even if the laws she was defending remained unchanged. "That should have been her position all along," George told me. "You know, that's politicians. That's how they play their games."

Their primary concern, as coverage of the exchange dominated radio call-in programs in the days that followed, was that it would further inflame the debate that Johnson had started. Specifically, they worried that the same people who had made names for themselves railing against LGBT rights the last time it was a high-profile issue would raise their voices again as the presidential campaign intensified. If this happened, all twenty presidential candidates might be tempted to weigh in.

After all, for politicians like Johnson, mining homophobia for votes is a far easier political strategy than devising and selling voters on a platform that would tackle Liberia's most difficult security and development challenges. "All of that is too much work, so they go directly to, 'This is what you hate, this is what I hate, so I could be your president,'" says Korto Williams, former country director of the anti-poverty organization ActionAid Liberia. "That is something that can be used as a currency."

As a result, one year on from the first round of voting, Liberian sexual minorities were preparing themselves for a perilous election season. "I'm sure that in the community there are conversations that are going on," Williams said at the time. "There is growing fear."

* * *

At first glance, there were signs that this fear was justified. When asked, the public figures who had driven the debate about LGBT rights in 2012 seemed as committed as ever to, at the very least, maintaining the status quo in Liberia.

In some cases, they claimed they would seize any opportunity, including that provided by a presidential campaign, to make the country more repressive. Rev. Kortu Brown, a prominent member of the New Citizens Movement who in 2012 had helped organize that group's petition drive and campaign against same-sex marriage, told me in early 2017 that he remained wary of the threat LGBT rights activists posed to "traditional culture." When I asked whether this view was widespread and how it might influence the campaign, Brown responded, "Any candidate who espouses gay marriage as a campaign tool will have a shock of their lives."

Yet these same public figures, Brown included, seemed at times to be merely going through the motions; on close inspection, their commitment to ridding Liberia of sexual minorities revealed itself to be fairly hollow. In the previous few years, the New Citizens Movement itself, despite Brown's rhetoric, had moved on from its earlier, almost singular focus on LGBT issues. At the height of the Ebola crisis, it had begun organizing group fasts and prayer sessions to raise awareness about the disease, and once the epidemic ended it had turned its attention to anti-poverty and anti-hunger initiatives.

And while, in his interview with me, Brown warned candidates against pushing for the legalization of same-sex marriage, the fact is that this goal had never been on the agenda of even the most ambitious LGBT rights activists, to say nothing of the presidential aspirants—something Brown surely knew. As Election Day drew closer, Brown seemed focused more than anything on trying to promote a peaceful democratic process and prevent the tensions of the political season from spilling over into violence.

"Liberia is at a critical point in our national life," he said.

> After the war, after Ebola, something's about to happen in Liberia that has not happened for seventy-three years. We have not had a sitting elected president transfer power to another elected president in seventy-three years. It's something that all of us, as a people, should be excited about and engaged with. How do we ensure that this historic democratic transition takes place in Liberia?

During a subsequent interview, Brown seemed to acknowledge that sexual minorities were not the threat his organization had once portrayed them as being. "We're still engaged with all the issues," he insisted. But in the next breath, he said, "I think that there are greater issues here to engage."

Among the candidates, no one other than Johnson made an effort to highlight LGBT rights as something that should concern voters. For this reason, the issue never achieved the same level of political urgency it had in 2012, instead resurfacing only sporadically. For example, shortly after he announced his candidacy, Alexander Cummings, a former Coca-Cola company executive and a political newcomer, weathered a series of newspaper articles suggesting that, perhaps because of his time spent working in the US, he was a supporter of gay rights and even same-sex marriage.

The basis for these articles was unclear. Cummings claimed they represented a "smear campaign" against him, and he tried to refute them whenever he could. "From a personal perspective, it's not a lifestyle that I encourage, that I support as a Christian," he said when I interviewed him at his campaign headquarters. At the same time, he said discrimination should not be tolerated in Liberia, and that, in any case, Liberian voters he met while campaigning were more concerned with issues like poverty.

Then he said something that, perhaps inadvertently, touched on the extent to which even relatively tolerant politicians are boxed in when it comes to LGBT rights, while subtly hinting at the potential for change down the road. "If you want to lead a people, you have to lead people to some extent where they need to go," he said, "but you also have to meet people where they are. And I'm meeting Liberians where they are."

Even Prince Johnson, who had come out swinging on LGBT rights in the early weeks of the campaign, appeared to tire of the issue. By the time I interviewed him, some eight months out from the first round of voting, he needed reminding that he had ever cared about it at all.

The interview took place in a cramped corner office on the second floor of a school he had built, not far from his Monrovia residence. Sitting behind a wooden teacher's desk, Johnson shouted instructions to aides who came in periodically, sometimes handing them bills from a wad of cash he kept in a drawer.

He and I had met six years earlier, during the 2011 campaign, and when I mentioned this he immediately turned the conversation to his lingering grievances from that cycle. "The 2011 election, it was characterized by manipulations," he said. "Truly speaking, Madame Sirleaf did not win the 2011 election. She did not."

Thus began an extended rant on Sirleaf's various short-comings; the corrupt nature of Americo-Liberians and the ruling class in general; the disenfranchisement of indigenous Liberians; and the flawed interventions of Western donors. Even on that final point, LGBT rights did not come up until I specifically asked about it. When I did, Johnson took the opportunity to lavish praise on US President Donald Trump, who had drawn attention in Liberia for, among other reasons, media reports that his administration had removed LGBT-specific content from government websites.

Trump was clearly someone whom Johnson had come to admire. "The gay rights, he called it off," Johnson said.

"He dissolved it! And it will never come here—officially, no. We know that in every country you got some bad people, but officially no."

Johnson also reprised the 2012-era claim that Hillary Clinton had wanted to make foreign assistance conditional on the expansion of LGBT rights. "If she had won, they will deprive us of loan, of grant, of aid because they tie gay rights to human rights and they say it's a human rights violation. So we thank God that it's been dissolved," he said, chuckling a little. "I've succeeded. God succeeded. I've been edified, and God's been glorified."

Later on, though, Johnson claimed that LGBT rights was not something he had ever made central to his campaign. "Gay rights is not in our platform," he said. And while this was demonstrably false, it's also worth noting that, in the final months before voting, the issue did not come up again.

Fatu, the office manager at SAIL, says she was not surprised that the debate about LGBT rights fizzled out so quickly in 2016 and 2017. "Here in Liberia, people tend to focus on some stuff for some time and then later on people just forget it," she says. "So we talk about stuff here but then again as time goes by it just blows over. At that time, in that moment, I was worried, but I knew with time it was going to blow over and it was just going to be something that he said at that time, so I wasn't worried about the future."

Patrick, the founder of SAIL, agreed. He said, "I knew that it was just the regular issue of politicians using tactics in their own way of distracting from development issues and the reality of society."

* * *

In the months immediately following Johnson's initial invocation of "Sodom and Gomorrah," however, it was by no means clear that his attempt to turn Liberians against sexual minorities wouldn't resonate with the public and become something bigger, potentially resulting in violence or threats of violence. As Liberian LGBT rights activists remembered all too well, the crisis in 2012 had been a complete surprise, highlighting the unpredictable nature of shifts in public opinion.

As they braced themselves for a similar scenario, these activists realized that they were better prepared this time, and that they could, in many ways, build on the work they'd already been doing over the previous few years. They had also learned by that point how to use the engagement of foreign governments, the US included, to their advantage, profiting from the contacts and resources those governments provided.

When it came to ramping up security training and reminding sexual minorities how to keep themselves out of danger, SAIL benefited from the fact that its new office, the one in Mamba Point, was located in a secure, gated compound. Members of SAIL and other sexual minorities were comfortable going there even during a time of heightened tension, and SAIL's leaders were confident that any training sessions they organized would not be disrupted by outsiders. This was a far cry from 2012, when the fact that SAIL lacked a safe headquarters meant its members were forced to disperse and fend for themselves as threats to their security mounted.

Patrick says SAIL's members were also able to take advantage of contacts in the media to ensure that coverage of Johnson's campaign launch did not devolve into negative reporting about sexual minorities in general. That the coverage remained largely focused on candidates' positions reflected how public discourse about sexual minorities had softened since 2012, in no small part thanks to SAIL's media outreach.

Additionally, by 2017 activists were established and emboldened enough to continue with their programming rather than allow bursts of hostility to cow them into silence. In Fatu's case, that meant going ahead with a Pride Month fundraising event and inviting journalists to cover it. "We did a couple of interviews and it went on the radio and there was some stuff on blogs that people wrote," Fatu says. "And we got a positive response. There was not much backlash. There were a few of the usual people saying, 'LGBT, oh, we don't want them here,' you know. But that was it."

Lastly, activists continued their work with the government, having concluded that it was essential to stay engaged with those responsible for shaping state policy.

One afternoon in early 2017, a group of around twenty gay and transgender Liberians crowded around a conference table in the stuffy basement of a government ministry in central Monrovia. As representatives of various organizations engaged in the fight against HIV/AIDS, they had been selected to work as peer educators, meaning they would soon be traveling around the country bearing information intended to bring down the sky-high transmission rates in their communities.

Much of the workshop covered technical information about sexually transmitted diseases and the reproductive system. But the frequent singing, occasional shouting, open flirting and frank discussions of gay sex indicated that participants were getting something else out of the day: an opportunity to come together in a space unmarred by the homophobia and transphobia they might encounter on city streets. The fact that this was all taking place in a ministry building, a symbol of the state that outlaws the very sex they were describing, was a sign of how far Liberia's LGBT movement had come since 2012.

Yet there were also plenty of reminders of how far they were from full acceptance. As the day wound down, participants were handed yellow sticky notes and instructed to write their fears and goals. Karishma, the facilitator, then read those anonymous submissions aloud as the room listened in silence: "Hate speech." "Too much overacting when we're outside." "I don't want to become insecure." "How do I make a new friend?" "My fear is to be exposed or arrested by police." "Not to be showing off." "Not to die alone."

As they work toward building a Liberia in which those fears can be conquered and those wishes fulfilled, Liberian activists say they are heeding the two most important lessons that can be gleaned from their experiences since 2011, when the Obama administration's memorandum promoting LGBT rights thrust them into the national spotlight for the first time. They are lessons that can also be applied elsewhere on the continent.

The first is that the homophobia and hatred they are trying to counter—whether stoked by politicians like Prince Johnson, religious leaders like Kortu Brown or ordinary Liberians—is often less formidable than it is portrayed as being. This is not to downplay the risks posed by public statements that demonize sexual minorities, or by populations that can sometimes be made to believe that sexual minorities are to blame for problems like poverty, bad schools and corruption. The number of individual horror stories in Liberia alone—going back to the killing of Tecumsay Roberts, the Liberian Michael Jackson, and continuing to present-day reports of assault, harassment and family rejection—make it impossible to ever push those risks entirely out of one's mind. But the fallout from Prince Johnson's campaign launch underscored how public anger at sexual minorities, however easy to incite, tends to rest on flimsy foundations and is therefore difficult to sustain. Before long, people are naturally inclined to turn their attention to issues that actually shape their day-to-day lives.

The second lesson, which their counterparts in Cameroon and Côte d'Ivoire have also proved, is that African activists are better positioned to navigate flare-ups of homophobia in their own countries than outsiders often give them credit for. External interventions, especially when it comes to marshaling support from the diplomatic community, can certainly be helpful in emergencies, but they are ultimately far less meaningful than the slow, deliberate work performed by local activists both in times of crisis and in periods of relative calm.

* * *

Of course, local activists can't afford to focus exclusively on what's happening in their own countries. They must also remain attuned to how shifts in global politics might influence the types of resources and assistance made available by their partners abroad. For this reason, even as they were figuring out how best to navigate Liberia's 2017 presidential campaign, members of SAIL and other Liberian sexual minorities were closely monitoring the changing political winds on the other side of the Atlantic Ocean, in the United States.

Many of these activists had been open about their hope that the winner of the US presidential election would be Hillary Clinton, who, while slow to champion LGBT rights domestically, had become a vocal supporter of them during her time at the State Department. After Trump won instead, these activists feared an immediate drop in material and moral support. In the days after the results were announced, as he processed the news, George, the SAIL activist, said he worried first about cuts for the Global Fund to Fight AIDS, Tuberculosis and Malaria, to which the US is the biggest contributor. He grew increasingly troubled as he watched the White House let Pride Month in 2017 pass by unacknowledged, and as Trump called for a ban on transgender people serving in the military.

Many Liberians, George says, view such measures as indicators that LGBT rights are no longer a matter of concern for Washington even at home, much less in a place like Liberia. While they remained hopeful that they could continue to count on the US as an ally, they were also aware that backing from the Trump administration, which has proposed cutting diplomacy and aid budgets by a third, was not guaranteed.

Not everyone was despondent over this. Fatu says that regardless of the decisions made by US officials, the influence of American culture would continue to push Liberians toward tolerance. She cites the TV series *Empire*, a hit in Liberia, and its gay character Jamal Lyon, played by Jussie Smollett, as an example of the type of visibility that she believes is changing minds.

But those working in development in Liberia say that no amount of television exposure would make up for the loss of State Department leadership on the issue. "In Liberia, we're not that many donors. We're very, very, very few," says Elisabeth Harleman, deputy head of mission at the

Swedish Embassy, one of the top bilateral donors behind the United States. It's difficult to imagine how programming would not be affected if the proposed funding cuts were approved. "We hope that other donors will come in and cover, but who are those other donors?"

For many African LGBT rights activists, not just in Liberia, dependence on foreign funding is one of the biggest problems facing their movements, and their concerns go well beyond the fact that this funding can be inconsistent. In an essay published in May 2016, the activists Liesl Theron, John McCallister and Mariam Armisen outlined several ways in which the outsize influence of foreign donors prevents African sexual minority activist movements from being as responsive as possible to the people they're trying to serve. For one thing, they wrote, it creates inequalities within movements by privileging activists who have received formal education and can operate effectively in the colonial languages of French and English. It also fosters the type of competition for resources that discourages collaboration and creates situations in which work is "happening in silos."

More fundamentally, there's an inevitable tension when the interests of donors and the needs of African sexual minorities don't fully overlap, a dynamic that, over the years, has led to gross imbalances, notably the fact that men who have sex with men are privileged over groups that were less affected by the HIV/AIDS epidemic.

The question going forward, then, is how to devise alternative funding models in which LGBT activists are better placed to sustain themselves, or to least be able to assert greater control over the direction of their own movements. For the moment, there are no obvious answers. Fatu is convinced that, in the short term at least, the reliance on foreign donors will have to continue. "I'm not sure Africans will be willing to support anything that has to do with a gay or whatever," she says. "I don't think so."

Yet others are more upbeat about the prospect of solving the problem of how to build a movement that can stand on its own. Perhaps they simply have to be. The solutions, which will inevitably be of their own making, will determine whether and how they can keep doing their life's work while experiencing some semblance of financial security.

"I'm very practical in my approach. I very much appreciate the foreign donors, and I thank those who have supported our cause," says one such activist, Cyriaque, an Ivorian who has worked throughout West Africa.

More than anything, though, Cyriaque says he is looking forward to solving the thorniest questions related to the movement's next chapter: how to be as inclusive as possible, how to be more self-sufficient; how, in short, to create the conditions that will allow activists like himself to prevail in the long run. "I think," he says, "that we need to work toward finding our own champions."

Selected Interviews

Andrews, Necus, Monrovia, February 2017

Banks, Andre, phone interview, November 2014

Behen, Parfait, Doula, February 2016

Beyoncé, Monrovia, February 2017

Bonnet, Guillaume, phone interview, November 2014

Brahima, series of interviews conducted in Abidjan and
    Yamoussoukro between June 2014 and December 2016

Cyriaque, Monrovia, February 2017

David, Abidjan, October 2014.

Daygbor, E.J. Nathaniel, Monrovia, January 2012

Didier, Yaoundé, June 2015

Evina, Brice, Yaoundé, February 2016

Fatu, series of interviews conducted in Monrovia, February 2017

Freida, Patience, Douala, November 2014

Gueboguo, Charles, phone interview, July 2015

Harleman, Elisabeth, Monrovia, February 2017

Harmony, Monrovia, February 2017

Johnson, Cary Alan, Skype interview, February 2016

Jules, Yaoundé, July 2015

Kamden, Paul, Yaoundé, February 2016

Karishma, Monrovia, February 2017

Kumche, Peter, Yaoundé, February 2016.

Kwame, Monrovia, February 2017

Lambert, series of interviews conducted in Yaoundé between
    December 2014 and August 2017

Lapar, Thomas Fouquet, phone interview, November 2014

Mekella, Monrovia, February 2017

Nguyen, Vinh-Kim, phone interview, January 2015

Nkom, Alice, Douala, November 2014

Nkurikiye, Jean-Eric, phone interview, November 2014

Noel, Yaoundé, November 2014

Patrick, series of interviews conducted in Monrovia and over the
    phone between February 2017 and July 2018

Reid, Graeme, phone interview, November 2014

Simon, Yaoundé, July 2015

Stéphane, Yaoundé, June 2015 and February 2016

Togué, Michel, Yaoundé, November 2014

Williams, Korto, phone interview, September 2017

References

Amnesty International, 2009. "Cameroun: L'impunité favorise les atteintes constantes aux droits humaines." January. https://www.amnesty.org/download/Documents/44000/afr170012009fra.pdf

Associated Press, 2014 "Gay man jailed in Cameroon has died, says lawyer," Jan. 13. Accessed via The Guardian: https://www.theguardian.com/world/2014/jan/13/gay-man-jailed-cameroon-died-lawyer-mbedees

Azango, Mae, 2018. "Liberia: Tecumsay Roberts and music icons slain in war, to be honored at industry awards." *FrontPage Africa*. Dec. 21.

BBC, 2011. "Cameron threat to dock some UK aid to anti-gay nations." Oct. 30. https://www.bbc.com/news/uk-15511081

Berkeley, Bill, 1992. "Liberia." *The Atlantic*. December. https://www.theatlantic.com/magazine/archive/1992/12/liberia/376354/

Brooks, Philip and Laurent Bocahut, 1998. *Woubi Chéri*. San Francisco: California Newsreel.

CBC News, 2016. "Trudeau asked about women and LGBTQ rights in Liberia." Nov. 24. https://www.youtube.com/watch?v=lY_dusVoKFc

Center for Constitutional Rights, 2017. "In scathing ruling, court
affirms SMUG's charges against U.S. anti-gay extremist Scott
Lively while dismissing on jurisdictional ground." June 6.
https://ccrjustice.org/home/press-center/press-releases/
scathing-ruling-court-affirms-smug-s-charges-against-us-anti-gay

Clinton, Hillary, 2011. "Remarks in recognition of International
Human Rights Day." Dec. 6. https://2009-2017.state.gov/
secretary/20092013clinton/rm/2011/12/178368.htm

Corey-Boulet, Robbie, 2014. "Giving a voice and nuanced
understanding to gay rights in West African media."
OPENSpace. November. http://www.osiwa.org/
wp-content/uploads/2015/08/LGBTI-Rights.pdf

Corey-Boulet, Robbie, 2015. "Who Killed Roger Mbede?"
Al-Jazeera, March 26. http://america.aljazeera.com/
articles/2015/3/26/who-killed-roger-mbede-gay-rights-
cameroon.html

Corey-Boulet, Robbie, 2016. "Liberia sees a backlash against gay
rights ahead of next year's election." *World Politics Review.*
Oct. 27.

Currier, Ashley and Joëlle M. Cruz, 2017. "The politics of
pre-emption: mobilisation against LGBT rights in Liberia."
Social Movement Studies. April.

Daygbor, E.J. Nathaniel, 2012. "53rd legislature to pass gay bill
for US $4m?" *New Dawn.* Jan. 9.

Ellis, Stephen, 2001. *The Mask of Anarchy: The Destruction of
Liberia and the Religious Dimension of an African Civil War.*
London: Hurst.

Epprecht, Marc, 2008. *Heterosexual Africa? The History of an
Idea from the Age of Exploration to the Age of AIDS.* Athens,
OH: Ohio University Press.

Erasing 76 Crimes, 2013. "Cameroon groups: it's too dangerous
to keep fighting AIDS." July 22. https://76crimes.com/

2013/07/22/cameroon-groups-its-too-dangerous-to-keep-fighting-aids/

Erasing 76 Crimes, 2016. "Anti-gay Cameroonians target LGBTI rights activists." July 7. https://76crimes.com/2016/07/07/anti-gay-cameroonians-target-lgbti-rights-activists/

Evans-Pritchard, E.E., 1937. *Witchcraft, oracles and magic among the Zande*. Oxford: Oxford University Press.

Ford, Tamasin and Bonnie Allen, 2012. "Nobel peace prize winner defends law criminalising homosexuality in Liberia." *The Guardian*. March 19.

Fraternité Matin, 1998. "Octobre 1998: Mois de la pédophilie. Plus de 50 fois à 'la une' des journaux." Nov. 3.

Gaudio, Rudolf Pell, 2009. *Allah Made Us: Sexual Outlaws in an Islamic African City*. Malden, MA: Wiley-Blackwell.

Gay, Judith, 1985. "'Mummies and babies' and friends and lovers in Lesotho." *Journal of Homosexuality* 11, no. 3–4: 97–116.

Ghoshal, Neela, 2013. "Processing the murder of Eric Ohena Lembembe." *The Daily Beast*. July 17. https://www.thedailybeast.com/processing-the-murder-of-eric-ohena-lembembe

Gueboguo, Charles, 2006. *La question homosexuelle en Afrique: Le cas du Cameroun*. Paris: L'Harmattan.

Horton, Stephanie C., 2012. "Sexuality, identity and LGBT rights in Liberia: illegal and invisible." *African Arguments*. Jan. 31.

Human Rights Watch, 2010. "Criminalizing identities: rights abuses in Cameroon based on sexual orientation and gender identity." Nov. 4. https://www.hrw.org/report/2010/11/04/criminalizing-identities/rights-abuses-cameroon-based-sexual-orientation-and#

Human Rights Watch, 2013. "Cameroon: spate of attacks on human rights defenders." July 1. https://www.hrw.org/news/2013/07/01/cameroon-spate-attacks-rights-defenders

Human Rights Watch and Amnesty International, 2014.
"Uganda: anti-homosexuality act's heavy toll." May 14.
https://www.hrw.org/news/2014/05/14/uganda-anti-
homosexuality-acts-heavy-toll

Human Rights Watch et al., 2005. "Letter to the Minister of
Justice of Cameroon regarding 11 men detained on suspicion
of homosexual activity." Nov. 30. https://www.hrw.org/
news/2005/11/30/letter-minister-justice-cameroon-
regarding-11-men-detained-suspicion-homosexual

Human Rights Watch, 2013. "'It's nature, not a crime':
discriminatory laws and LGBT people in Liberia." Dec.

International Crisis Group, 2010. "Cameroon: the dangers of a
fracturing regime." June 24. https://www.crisisgroup.org/
africa/central-africa/cameroon/cameroon-dangers-
fracturing-regime

International Crisis Group, 2011. "Liberia: how sustainable is
the recovery?" Aug. 19.

International Gay and Lesbian Human Rights Commission
(IGLHRC), 2005. "Cameroon: IGLHRC calls on Minister of
Justice to release 11 men unfairly detained in jail." Dec. 5.https:
//www.outrightinternational.org/content/cameroon-iglrhc-
calls-minister-justice-release-11-men-unfairly-detained-jail

International Gay and Lesbian Human Rights Commission
(IGLHRC), 2006. "Cameroon: nine men acquitted in major
victory for human rights!" April 21. https://www.
outrightinternational.org/content/cameroon-nine-men-
acquitted-major-victory-human-rights

Johnson, Cary Alan, 2007. *Off the Map: How HIV/AIDS
Programming Is Failing Same-Sex Practicing People in
Africa*. New York: IGLHRC. https://www.opensociety
foundations.org/sites/default/files/Off%2520the%
2520Map.pdf

Jonassen, Wendi, 2014. "Bay area man plants rainbow flag on tallest mountain in Uganda." KQED. May 2. https://www.kqed.org/news/134972/bay-area-man-plants-rainbow-flag-on-tallest-mountain-in-uganda

Kaoma, Kapya, 2009/10. "The U.S. Christian Right and the attack on gays in Africa." *The Public Eye Magazine*. Winter/Spring.

Le Pape, Marc and Claudine Vidal, 1984. "Libéralisme et vécus sexuels à Abidjan." *Cahiers internationaux de sociologie*, 16: 111–118.

Mandel, Jean-Jacques, 1983. "L'Afrique de l'an 2000?" *Libération*. Jan. 11.

Metzger, Céline, 2009. *Cameroun: Sortir du Nkuta*. Nantes: Les Films du Balibari.

Muhumuza, Rodney, 2014. "2 Ugandans go on trial over homosexual offenses." The Associated Press. May 7. https://www.washingtonexaminer.com/2-ugandans-go-on-trial-over-homosexual-offenses

Murray, Stephen O. and Will Roscoe, 1998. *Boy-Wives and Female Husbands: Studies in African Homosexualities*. London: Palgrave Macmillan.

Naipaul, V.S., 1984. "The Crocodiles of Yamoussoukro." *The New Yorker*. May 14.

Ndjio, Basile, 2012. "Post-colonial histories of sexuality: the political invention of a libidinal African straight." *Africa: The Journal of the International African Institute*, 82, no. 4: 609–631.

Nguyen, Vinh-Kim, 2005. "Uses and pleasures: sexual modernity, HIV/AIDS, and confessional technologies in a West African metropolis." In *Sex in Development: Science, Sexuality and Morality in Global Perspective*, edited by Stacy Leigh Pigg and Vincanne Adams. Durham, NC: Duke University Press.

Nguyen, Vinh-Kim, 2010. *The Republic of Therapy: Triage and Sovereignty in West Africa's Time of AIDS*. Durham, NC: Duke University Press.

Noble, Kenneth B., 1994. "French devaluation of African currency brings wide unrest." *The New York Times*. Feb. 23. https://www.nytimes.com/1994/02/23/world/french-devaluation-of-african-currency-brings-wide-unrest.html

Nyeck, S.N. "Mobilizing against the invisible: erotic nationalism, mass media, and the 'paranoid style' in Cameroon." *From Sexual Diversity in Africa: Politics, Theory and Citizenship*, edited by S.N. Nyeck and Marc Epprecht. Montreal: McGill-Queen's University Press. 2013.

Perelman, Marc and Johan Bodin, 2014. "Cameroon: where being gay is a crime." France 24. Jan. 1. https://www.france24.com/en/20140117-reporters-cameroon-plight-homosexuals-gay-rights-prison-deaths

Pflanz, Mike, 2011. "Africa reacts to Obama's pro-gay rights foreign policy." *The Christian Science Monitor*. Dec. 8.

Presidential Memorandum, 2011. "Presidential Memorandum—International Initiatives to Advance the Human Rights of Lesbian, Gay, Bisexual, and Transgender Persons." Dec. 6. https://obamawhitehouse.archives.gov/the-press-office/2011/12/06/presidential-memorandum-international-initiatives-advance-human-rights-l

Reid, Graeme, 2013. *How to Be a Real Gay: Gay Identities in Small-Town South Africa*. Pietermaritzburg, South Africa: University of KwaZulu-Natal Press.

Remarks, 2013. "Remarks by President Obama and President Sall of the Republic of Senegal at Joint Press Conference." June 27. https://obamawhitehouse.archives.gov/the-press-office/2013/06/27/remarks-president-obama-and-president-sall-republic-senegal-joint-press-

SAIL et al., 2014. "Human rights violations against lesbian, gay, bisexual, and transgender (LGBT) people in Liberia: a shadow report on Liberia's compliance with the African Charter on Human and Peoples' Rights." April–May. https://www.heartlandalliance.org/gihr/wp-content/uploads/sites/12/2016/07/ACHPR-Liberia-Alternative-Report-2014.pdf

Sieh, Rodney D., 2016. "The big issues that should decide Liberia's 2017 presidential race." *FrontPage Africa*. Aug. 3.

Soir Info, 1998. "Pédophilie en Côte d'Ivoire: les Ivoiriens condamnent et réclament justice." Oct. 7.

Southern Poverty Law Center, n.d. "Scott Lively." https://www.splcenter.org/fighting-hate/extremist-files/individual/scott-lively

Southern Poverty Law Center, 2009. "U.S. anti-gay leaders holding seminar in Uganda." March 6. https://www.splcenter.org/hatewatch/2009/03/06/us-anti-gay-leaders-holding-seminar-uganda

Theron, Liesl, John McAllister and Mariam Armisen, 2016. "Where do we go from here? A call for critical reflection on queer/LGBTIA+ activism in Africa." May 12. https://www.pambazuka.org/gender-minorities/where-do-we-go-here

Thomann, Matthew, 2014. *The Price of Inclusion: HIV, sexual subjectivity, and belonging in Abidjan, Côte d'Ivoire.* PhD dissertation, American University.

Thomann, Matthew, 2016. "HIV vulnerability and the erasure of sexual and gender diversity in Abidjan, Côte d'Ivoire." *Global Public Health* 11, no. 7–8: 994–1009.

Thomann, Matthew and Robbie Corey-Boulet, 2015. "Violence, exclusion and resilience among Ivoirian *travesties*." *Critical African Studies* 9, no. 1: 106–123.

Thoreson, Ryan R., 2014. *Transnational LGBT Activism: Working for Sexual Rights Worldwide*. Minneapolis: University of Minnesota Press.

UN, 2006. François Ayissi et al. v. Cameroon, Working Group on Arbitrary Detention, Opinion No. 22/2006, UN Doc. A/HRC/4/40/Add.1 at 91 (2006). http://hrlibrary.umn.edu/wgad/22-2006.html

UN, 2013. "Cameroon, UPR Report Consideration—24th Meeting 24th Regular Session of Human Rights Council." UN Web TV. Sept. 20. http://webtv.un.org/en/ga/watch/cameroon-upr-report-consideration-24th-meeting-24th-regular-session-of-human-rights-council/2682873093001/?term=&page=6?lanfrench

UNAIDS, 2013. "Global AIDS Response Progress Reporting (GARPR) 2013, Country Progress Report, Republic of Liberia." http://www.unaids.org/sites/default/files/country/documents/LBR_narrative_report_2014.pdf

US Department of State, 2003. *Country Reports on Human Rights Practices—Cameroon*. March 21. https://www.state.gov/j/drl/rls/hrrpt/2002/18172.htm

Vidal, Claudine, 1977. "Guerre des sexes à Abidjan. Masculin, féminin, CFA." *Cahiers d'études africaines*, 17, no. 65: 121–153.

Notes

Introduction

1   Like many of the people described and quoted in this book, David's name has been changed to protect his identity.

Chapter 1

1   'Yaoundé 11' case file provided by Alice Nkom, reviewed in Douala in November 2014.

Chapter 2

1   IGLHRC changed its name to OutRight Action International in 2015.

Chapter 5

1   https://www.youtube.com/watch?v=lcTg0qrBMo0

Chapter 12

1   For security reasons, Patrick, whose name has been changed, asked that certain details of his story, including the West African country where he sought refuge during Liberia's wars, be omitted.

Index

background, 210; HIV/
AIDS, 237, 278; Operation
Octopus, 228; Providence
Baptist Church, 221;
rebellion, 228, 265–267;
SAIL (Stop AIDS in
Liberia), 238, 243–244; sex
workers, 251; US Embassy,
215
Mount Stanley, Uganda, 5
Movement Against Gays in
Liberia *see* MOGAL
Movement for Defense of Gays
and Lesbians in Liberia *see*
MODEGAL
MSM (men who have sex with
men) *see* gay men
Mugabe, Robert, 46–47, 207
Murray, Stephen O. and
Roscoe, Will, 40–41, 42, 51
Museveni, Yoweri, 5–6, 9, 208

Nagenda, John, 208
Naipaul, V.S., 188
Nana, Joel, 32, 34
National Chronicle
(newspaper), 205
National Patriotic Front of
Liberia *see* NPFL
nationalism, 65
Nazism, 230
Ndjio, Basile, 66–67, 69

New Bell prison, Douala, 83
New Citizens Movement,
Liberia, 231–232, 271
New Dawn (newspaper), 2
03–204, 205
The New York Times
(newspaper), 121
The News (newspaper), 240
Nguyen, Vinh-Kim: on
Abidjan, 117–118; on
defamation case, 136;
on elites, 121, 125, 127;
on HIV/AIDS, 169; on
terminology, 168; on
travestis, 172
Nigeria, 43, 258
Nkom, Alice, 24, 32–34, 37–
38, 48, 75, 78, 90–91
Nkurikiye, Jean-Eric, 92, 94
Noble, Kenneth B., 121
NPFL (National Patriotic
Front of Liberia), 223–224
Nyeck, S.N., 65, 68, 69, 70–71

Obama, Barack, 12, 176, 206,
208–211, 213, 229
organizations, international,
47–48
Ouattara, Alassane, 174–175

Pangwe ethnic group, 51
Paris, 111, 163

ZED

Zed is a platform for marginalised voices across the globe.

It is the world's largest publishing collective and a world leading example of alternative, non-hierarchical business practice.

It has no CEO, no MD and no bosses and is owned and managed by its workers who are all on equal pay.

It makes its content available in as many languages as possible.

It publishes content critical of oppressive power structures and regimes.

It publishes content that changes its readers' thinking.

It publishes content that other publishers won't and that the establishment finds threatening.

It has been subject to repeated acts of censorship by states and corporations.

It fights all forms of censorship.

It is financially and ideologically independent of any party, corporation, state or individual.

Its books are shared all over the world.

www.zedbooks.net
@ZedBooks